# Destination Unknown

## Sustainable Travel and Ethical Tourism

---

*Edited by*
Carolin Lusby

# Destination Unknown

## Sustainable Travel and Ethical Tourism

*Edited by*
Carolin Lusby

COMMON
GROUND

First published in 2021
as part of the *Tourism and Leisure Studies* Book Imprint
doi: 10.18848/978-1-86335-238-3/CGP (Full Book)

Common Ground Research Networks
60 Hazelwood Drive
University of Illinois Research Park
Champaign, IL
61820

Library of Congress Cataloging-in-Publication Data

Names: Lusby, Carolin, editor.
Title: Destination unknown : sustainable travel and ethical tourism /
    edited by Carolin Lusby.
Other titles: Destination unknown (Common Ground Publishing)
Description: Champaign, IL : Common Ground, 2021. | Includes
    bibliographical references. | Summary: "Reflecting on the industry in a
    historical stand still offers a unique opportunity to rethink what is
    important in life. As the world has hit a universal reset button, we are
    allowed to imagine a travel and tourism that is fair, balanced, and
    resilient. Uncontrolled mass tourism and over- tourism have proven to
    have many negative impacts on societies, people, economies and
    environments. And while alternative forms of tourism have been shown to
    combat and mitigate some of these impacts, they are still niche markets.
    The tourism industry has the potential to take a leading role in
    fostering intercultural understandings, where local uniqueness and
    cultural diversity are both seen as assets, contributing to a memorable
    experience and excellent touristic product"-- Provided by publisher.
Identifiers: LCCN 2021006699 (print) | LCCN 2021006700 (ebook) | ISBN
    9780949313515 (hardback) | ISBN 9780949313980 (paperback) | ISBN
    9781863352369 (adobe pdf)
Subjects: LCSH: Sustainable tourism. | Tourism--Moral and ethical aspects.
Classification: LCC G156.5.S87 D48 2021  (print) | LCC G156.5.S87  (ebook)
    | DDC 174/.991--dc23
LC record available at https://lccn.loc.gov/2021006699
LC ebook record available at https://lccn.loc.gov/2021006700

Cover Photo Credit: Carolin Lusby

# Table of Contents

# Dedication

This book is dedicated to anyone who has felt the urge to connect to new lands and people in search of new horizons and soul growth. Now, more than ever, we are reminded that we are one planet earth and one human race.

# Notes on Contributors

**Allegra Celine Baumann** holds a master's degree in Sociology with a focus on Urban Sociology from Technische Universität (TU) Darmstadt, Germany. Currently, she is a PhD candidate and a research associate in the Research Training Group KRITIS (Critical Infrastructures) at the same institution. In her PhD research, she focuses on the impact of cruise tourism on technical urban infrastructure systems using as a case study the city of Dubrovnik, Croatia. In addition to her PhD, Allegra is doing her bachelor's degree in Environmental Engineering, working as a lecturer at several universities and as a freelance journalist for a culture magazine.

**Lisa Cain** is an Assistant Professor in the Chaplin School of Hospitality and Tourism Management at Florida International University, where she teaches undergraduate and graduate Hospitality Management courses. She earned her doctoral degree from the University of Nevada, Las Vegas in Hotel Administration, her Master's degree from Florida International University in Hospitality Management, and her Bachelor's degree from Smith College in English Language and Literature. She also spent a year studying at Oxford University in England. Dr. Cain's research interests emphasize understanding and exploring internal and external customer experiences in both domestic and international settings.

**Renita Ferreira** is Indian-Portuguese and has learned the world through multiple languages including English, French, Hindi, Arabic, and Spanish. Her love for travel started in Bahrain and 70 other countries subsequently. That helped her gain extensive knowledge about multiple cultures, and how relevant interculturalism is to a global society. Her achievement in education cannot be overlooked earning three Bachelors, two Masters, and a doctorate. Each of those closely aligned with teacher education and diversity. She is currently teaching at Miami Dade College and is always eager to share her experiences and knowledge with her students.

**Kathleen H. Fitzgerald** is a conservation leader recognized for her extensive experience in integrated large landscape conservation programs in Africa and North America. She has lived in Africa for 13 years. She is a senior member of Conservation Capital and focuses on increasing revenue for protected area management and wildlife conservation. Kathleen has helped create new conservation areas, improve management of protected areas, established innovative public, private partnerships with African Governments and led community conservation initiatives. She has completed dozens of conservation land transactions in the United States and Africa, has a Master's of Science Degree from the University of Vermont and is a member of IUCN's Tourism and Protected Areas Specialist Group and IUCN's Connectivity Specialist Group.

**Friederike Hertwig** is currently a PhD candidate in Sustainable Development and Diplomacy at EUCLID University. She received her bachelor's degree in Tourism Management and her master's in International Development. In 2015, her research was published in a policy paper "From Volunteering to Voluntourism" in conjunction with several non-profit organizations. She runs the website responsible-volunteering.com with three other team members. Originally from Germany, Friederike has lived in Miami since 2016 and runs the US business for a German manufacturer.

**Yen E. Lam-González**, Doctor in Economy, Enterprise and Tourism (2017) of the University of Las Palmas de Gran Canaria (Spain). Bachelor in Economics (2005) and MBA (2008) of the University of Havana, Cuba. Master in Integral Development of Tourism Destinations (2012) of the University of Las Palmas de Gran Canaria (ULPGC). She teaches at the ULPGC, the Autonomous University of Chile and at the University of Cartagena. Author of more than 30 publications (books, chapters and journal articles). Peer reviewer in ten journals and coordinator of numerous scientific events and RDI European Projects. She has participated in the Integral Tourism Development Strategy of the Old Havana, world heritage site, and in capacity building and other cooperation initiatives for the United Nations, World Bank and the Swiss Agency for Development and Cooperation (SDC).

**Javier de León**, PhD is a lecturer at the University of Las Palmas de Gran Canaria, Spain. His research interests center on tourism, sustainable development, social representations, cooperation, consumer behavior and destination management. He has published numerous manuscripts in scientific journals, both national and international, and is author of a significant number of books and book chapters on these subjects. He has participated in numerous national and international research and cooperation projects. He is member of the Institute of Tourism and Sustainable Economic Development (Tides) and Director of Cooperation in the Vice-Rector's Office for Internationalization and Cooperation of the University of Las Palmas de Gran Canaria.

**Carolin Lusby** holds a PhD in Tourism and Natural Resources from the University of Florida. She was granted a Fulbright Scholar Award in Brazil, where she consulted in community-based tourism and collaborated in various research projects. She is an Assistant Professor in Tourism at Florida International University's Chaplin School of Hospitality and Tourism Management where she oversees the tourism program. She is passionate about travel and connecting people to people while preserving natural and cultural resources.

**Hitesh Mehta** is one of the world's leading authorities, practitioners and researchers on holistic eco-planning and eco-design, and both the landscape architectural and architectural aspects of ecolodges. He owns and operates HM Design. He is the author of various chapters and books including:" Authentic Ecolodges."

**Natália Marques da Silva** is a Doctoral Candidate in Global & Sociocultural Studies at Florida International University. Her research focuses on memory, heritage, and travel, as well as representations and narratives of enslavement.

**Niurka Cruz Sosa** holds a Master in Tourism Management from the University of Havana (Cuba). She is Vice-Director of the Master Plan for the Integral Development of the Old Havana, as part of the Historian's Office of Havana City. Her main research areas are: Cultural tourism, Creative industries, Destination management, Heritage, Sustainability, Caribbean Region.

# Introduction

*Carolin Lusby*

When COVID interrupted life as we knew it, the international tourism industry came to an abrupt stop. Our interconnected world was suddenly devoid of travelers, airplanes, cruise ships, hotel stays and the exchange of people and goods. The unimaginable had happened: international borders were closed; tourist attractions were shut down. The Christ statue in Rio de Janeiro, a universal sign of peace, stood empty overlooking the city, Christ wearing a mask to remind people to stay safe.

As uncertainty about the future of the industry grew, I was certain of one thing: Travel is essential, and we will rebound! For as long as humans existed, we have traveled.

The tourism industry has survived world wars, SARS, the Swine flu, hurricanes, terror attacks, 9/11, natural disasters such as red tide, warming oceans, and political unrests. It seems to be resilient. Why? Because the needs for cultural exchange, to visit sites of beauty, to connect with fellow humans, to explore new sites and learn new skills are hard wired within us. It is the stuff the makes life worth living. It is a fundamental human right. It is vital for intercultural understanding, peace and fosters economic equality.

Reflecting on the industry in a historical stand still offers a unique opportunity to rethink what is important in life. As the world has hit a universal reset button, we are allowed to imagine a travel and tourism that is fair, balanced, and resilient. Uncontrolled mass tourism and over- tourism have proven to have many negative impacts on societies, people, economies and environments. And while alternative forms of tourism have been shown to combat and mitigate some of these impacts, they are still niche markets.

The tourism industry has the potential to take a leading role in fostering intercultural understandings, where local uniqueness and cultural diversity are both seen as assets, contributing to a memorable experience and excellent touristic product. To achieve this, the industry must confront the ways in which it can inadvertently produce meanings that exclude many from the narrative, by simplifying them into dominant, and commercial interpretations of culture and people. How then do we construct authentic and unique meanings and places, as we reflect on and design culture for tourism? How can the focus be on diverse experiences and direct human interactions, as opposed to the barriers created by tourism bubbles, such as mass resorts or cruise ships?

This book aims at answering these questions by investigating some of the current issues and trends in the industry, so as to offer solutions and visions for a new tourism beneficial to all. # Travel Tomorrow

What if we could redesign the industry to offer opportunities for learning, digital detox, deep connection to nature, each other and the universal force that connects us all? What if, through travel, we allow meaningful economic development and enhanced quality of life? What if through travel we deepen our understanding of each other and global solutions to global problems? A new consciousness of sustainability and an ethic that calls for tourism development that is good for local people, the traveler and the environment is what will make the industry more resilient and meaningful.

Chapter One discusses the issues of over-tourism, cruise tourism, authenticity, and Disneyfication. The chapter acknowledges that all tourism creates spaces of encounters, yet how we facilitate these makes a world of a difference. The author concludes that individualized tours that highlight authentic experiences are a means to create positive experiences of tourists and destinations.

Chapter Two highlights successful efforts of conservation through tourism in Africa, demonstrating that the cultural aspects of authentic engagement with local people in communities create meaningful experiences that keep visitors happy and returning. When these cultural encounters are linked to a wildlife product, it can extend the length of stay for tourists, enhance the tourism product, directly benefit local cultures and communities, and provide a meaningful cross-cultural experience that cultivates awareness about local cultures.

Chapter Three builds on the concepts of encounters and cultural tourism discussed in chapters one and two, and investigates loyalty of cultural travelers in Havana, Cuba. The chapter stresses that mass tourism, degradation of natural and cultural resources have a negative impact on return visits and hence need to be properly managed for successful cultural tourism.

Chapter Four expands the notion of cultural tourism to interculturalism in tourism, examining its meanings and implications in relation to intercultural connections such as tourist- host relations.

Chapter Five examines a special type of tourist- host encounter, which has been growing rapidly in popularity: volunteering in tourism. The chapter takes a critical look at the industry and shows how a focus on tourist demands and satisfactions can lead to unethical and dramatically damaging consequences. A rapid demand for giving back experiences led to a swift commodification of voluntourism, where shortcuts in selecting and controlling missions led to projects that are unbeneficial, and at times even harmful to the recipient (as in the case of some orphanage tourism programs). The chapter offers an outlook for ethical volunteering and offers resources for both organizations and travelers.

Chapter Six delves into the concept of ethical design and architecture in tourism ventures, by arguing for vernacular design as a means to achieve balanced, culturally appropriate and sustainable facility planning.

Chapter Seven investigates a particular form of ethnic tourism in which travelers revisit sites of enslavement to find meaning, roots and memories. This special form of connecting to other lands and peoples serves as a vehicle to confront contemporary legacies of oppression.

# Chapter 1

# Spaces for Encounters between Tourists and Locals in Times of Cruise Tourism and Overtourism

*Allegra Celine Baumann*
*Research Training Group KRITIS, TU*
*Darmstadt, Germany*

## Introduction

Modern times are characterized by high mobility of people and goods. Tourism plays an essential role in our mobile world. Due to its high value in and its impact on everyday life, as well as its importance for economies worldwide, it can be argued that we are living in 'the age of tourism' (D'Eramo, 2018; translation by author). Tourism changed over the last centuries. The times of the Grand Tour, in which traveling was reserved for a small elite, are outdated. Nowadays, an increasing amount of people worldwide spend their holidays abroad. The range of holiday offers is more diverse than ever: tourists can travel Russia using the Trans-Siberian Railway, go on an expedition to the Antarctic, climb Mount Everest, go Backpacking in Thailand, take an ocean cruise to the Caribbean or stay in an all-inclusive hotel at the Egyptian coast. Mass tourism and lower prices for long-distance travel result in yearly increasing tourist numbers. With 1.5 billion international tourist arrivals worldwide in 2019, numbers grew by 4% in comparison to the previous year (UNWTO, 2020). Tourism is of high importance in our modern world, not only due to its economic relevance, but because of its potential to foster intercultural understandings. When people travel to spend their holidays away from their home country, cross-border encounters between people are possible. By getting in contact with locals, tourists can experience realities, which differ from their own. In our modern, globalized and highly complicated world, "tourism matters, because it provides both a lens onto and an energy for relationships within everyday life" (Jack & Phipps, 2005). Hence, this chapter strives to answer the question how spaces for encounters between tourists and locals can be created in times of overtourism and cruise tourism, focusing on the role of authentic experiences.

## Authenticity in the Tourist Experience

Authenticity is one of the most well-known concepts in tourism research. Tourists are looking for authentic experiences to get in contact with locals, try local food, and see, purchase or even participate in local crafts and traditions. The demand for authenticity is a basic principle of tourism itself. Even in early travel reports like Mark Twain's *The Innocents Abroad* published in 1896, the tourists' demand for authentic experiences plays an essential role during the journey. In this report about his cruise travel, he describes his and his travel companions' impressions of Tangier:

> *Here is not the slightest thing that ever we have seen in pictures—and we always mistrusted the pictures before—they seemed too weird and fanciful for reality. But behold, they were not wild enough they have not told half the story.* (Twain, 1896 [2010], 47)

It becomes obvious that Twain and his travel companions compare the image of the foreign place, which they had in mind, with reality—with the purpose of having authentic experiences. The comparison of expectations and reality plays an important role for the evaluation of authentic experiences: "everything is there to be visited, recognized, and categorized with other images" (Lowry, 1991, 22). Hence, the way authenticity is evaluated, is strongly connected to previous knowledge and stereotypical images about visited destinations and cultures. In places that are designed for tourist purposes, these images are used to create a feeling of authenticity. Hence, there are multiple layers of authenticity, which are conceptualized by MacCannell (1976) as different stages of "Staged Authenticity" (see Knowledge Box 1).

Authentic experiences can take place in regard to places, things and people. Tourists visit famous historical sites and buildings, museums to see original works of popular artists or Native American villages to experience the way people live and work in these communities. Based on MacCannell's concept of "Staged Authenticity" the question arises, which stage tourists get to see and its role in creating spaces for encounters with locals. It is unlikely that tourists ever get to see stage six and have truly authentic experiences. Offers and tours for tourists are always staged, at least to a certain degree. However, an experience does not have to be truly authentic to create a space for encounters between tourists and locals. Tourists' demand for having authentic experiences and their hope to make a "stage six"-experience is essential for them to engage with locals and local culture. If local communities as well as tourist agencies manage to make offers that let tourists take part in stage four and five, tourists' needs will be satisfied and places for intercultural communication and encounters can be created. To analyse how encounters between locals and tourists are possible in times of overtourism and cruise tourism, authenticity should be understood in an "everyday sense of 'being honest'" (London, 2011, 187).

---

**Knowledge Box 1: MacCannell's Concept of "Staged Authenticity"**

Is there such a thing as authenticity in tourist experiences? MacCannell (1976) introduced the concept of "Staged Authenticity" in the field of tourism research. Based on Goffman's concept of front and back stages in people's everyday life, MacCannell identifies six stages of staged authenticity in tourism. Stage one is the touristic front region. This stage is created for tourist purposes only. Tourists do not expect and will not experience authenticity here. Hence, they try to overcome this stage. Stage two is a touristic front region, but there is an effort done to let it appear more "authentic" and hence more like a back region. MacCannell uses the example of a fish restaurant's decoration with fishnets on the wall. Stage three is a touristic front region, which is designed to appear completely like a back region. Examples are traditional Native American villages in Northern America, where tourists can experience the "authentic" way of living and working of these communities. But in fact, the whole experience is staged as the community dresses up in traditional clothes and performs a show to fulfil tourist expectations. However, tourists can be aware of this. Stage four is the first back region, which is open for tourists. To distinguish between stage three and stage four can be difficult. Stage five is a back region, which is open for special occasions, e.g., tourist tours, where locals open their homes for tourists. Stage six is the real back stage, where the authentic life of locals takes place—the stage tourists want to see.

---

## Overtourism

Growing tourist numbers create economic benefits for destinations, but there are also negative effects. These effects are recently summarized using the term "overtourism". The term came up in 2016 and has been used in public as well as in academic discussion since then (UNWTO, 2018). Nowadays, overtourism is one of the well-known terms in tourism research and debates about modern tourism. The UNWTO defines overtourism as:

> the impact of tourism on a destination, or parts thereof, that excessively influences perceived quality of life of citizens and/or quality of visitors' experiences in a negative way. (UNWTO 2018, 6)

Manifestations of overtourism can vary in destinations: a lack of affordable housing for locals and an increase in rents because flats are turned into tourist apartments; the disappearance of shops for daily necessities and instead the establishing of souvenir shops and tourist restaurants; peaks and high pressure on technical, net-bound urban infrastructure systems such as roads or the sewage system created by high tourist numbers lead to failures or breakdowns; as well as environmental issues due to exhaust gases from cars or cruise ships. In rural areas, the problems of overtourism mostly have to do with a lack of technical infrastructure systems to cope with high tourist numbers as well as the fragility of nature. Especially European cities are affected by overtourism as Europe has most tourist arrivals worldwide with 716.1 million in 2018 (UNWTO, 2020). Besides high tourist numbers, most European cities do exist for a long time. Hence, their infrastructure is in large parts historical, which means their streets and city centres are quite narrow. As overtourism does not per se involve huge amounts of tourists, limited space increases pressure. Not only tourists' bodies consume space, but also tables and chairs belonging to tourist restaurants, cafés and bars. Thereby, destinations lose public space for citizens to walk, meet, sit or play.

Venice, Barcelona, Dubrovnik and Amsterdam are popular examples for their struggle with overtourism. But not only urban areas are affected, also remote areas like fjords in Norway or nature parks like Plitvice Lakes in Croatia have to deal with the consequences of high visitor numbers. In highly overcrowded destinations, locals spring into action to show their disappointment. Citizens in several destinations found initiatives to claim their rights and organize demonstrations. In some destinations, locals express their discontent with more rigid measures like anti-tourist graffiti, e.g., "tourists go home"-graffiti or even attacks on tourists as it happened in Barcelona in 2017. These examples show that overtourism can lead to tension between locals and tourists.

Overtourism is often linked to cruise tourism, even though cruise tourism does not play a major role for all issues related to overtourism. Mostly, cruise tourism is mentioned in the context of overcrowding and environmental issues. The majority of destinations affected by overtourism, cities as well as remote areas such as villages in Norwegian fjords, are seaports. Cruise tourism is addressed by protests of citizens as well as in media reporting about overtourism, creating an image of the cruise ship as the symbol of overtourism. The contrast between the large cruise ships and the small buildings of ancient cities are used frequently as a visual expression of overtourism in mass media. The symbolic character of cruise ships in the overtourism debate is strengthened by the fact that they transport high numbers of tourists. These tourists arrive at the destination at the same time, visit the same sightseeing attractions, stay for a short, limited time, and usually spend a quite small amount of money. Hence, cruise tourism is symbolic for the tourism-related pressure on destinations. Furthermore, cruise passengers can be easily identified as they often pre-book their shore excursions with the cruise line and visit the destination in groups. Occasions for encounters between cruise tourists and locals are quite rare with this kind of shore excursions. However, most tourists look for encounters with locals and local culture while being on holidays. They want to have authentic experiences. Pre-booked shore excursions and the short length of stay in ports make it more difficult for cruise tourists to get in contact with locals.

## Cruise Tourism

Cruising has become one of the most popular forms of spending holidays and passenger numbers have increased constantly in the last ten years. Hence, the cruise tourism market has been growing rapidly in the last two decades (Dowling & Weeden, 2017; Ponton & Asero, 2018). Cruise tourism is one of the main growing tourism sectors with 28.5 million passengers in 2018 and an expected amount of 32 million passengers in 2020 (CLIA, 2018), which means that the percentage growth of the sector is higher than the percentage growth of tourism worldwide. Ocean cruises are operating worldwide, but the most popular region is the Caribbean, accommodating 32% of all cruise travels, followed by the Mediterranean with 17% (CLIA, 2018). The majority of cruise lines is organized with the Cruise Lines International Association (CLIA), which is with more than 50 members and more than 24 million yearly served passengers the main representative of the sector (CLIA, 2020).

As a result of the sector's growth, cruise lines order ships with higher passenger capacities. CLIA cruise lines will have 19 new ships debuting in 2021 (CLIA, 2020). One of vessel launched in 2020 is "Mardi Gras", accommodating up to 5200 passengers and thus Carnival Cruise Line's largest cruise ship regarding passenger capacities (CCL, 2020).

Ports have to take measures to deal with the growth of the cruise sector. One of these measures is the construction of new cruise terminals. In some cases, cruise terminals belong to the cruise lines themselves. Hence, cruise lines can design these terminals themselves as they take over all costs. Another measure is the improvement of the port infrastructure carried out by port authorities. An example is the cruise port in Dubrovnik, Croatia. The Port Authority initiated the straightening of the coastline to be able to accommodate larger cruise vessels. Hence, infrastructure improvement can be seen as a direct response to recent trends in the cruise sector which result in building vessels, which are bigger in size and have higher passenger capacities.

Besides the necessity for infrastructural improvements, port authorities also have to handle management aspects. Growing fleets result in more cruise ships calls at ports. In general, the amount of ships being handled simultaneously at ports has increased in the last years. As a result, seaports that are of tourist interest struggle with higher pressure due to the dilemma of having to accommodate greater numbers of cruise passengers (Morgan & Power, 2011). As a result, some port authorities decrease the numbers of cruise ships in the port, e.g., in Dubrovnik.

The cruise ship stay at a city's port is limited in time by the ship's schedule. In general, schedules of different cruise companies are similar as passengers want to stay at a destination during daytime when they visit the city's main attractions. The cruise ship travels from destination to destination during the night. Hence, most cruise ships stay at a destination at the same time during the day, which leads to a temporal and spatial concentration of cruise passengers in a city. Besides environmental issues, the concentration of passengers is one of the main reasons why cruise tourism is often addressed in the context of overtourism.

The huge amount of cruise passengers arriving at a destination at the same time as well as the pressure on infrastructure systems caused thereby can aggravate the negative perception of cruise tourism by locals; and therefore hamper encounters between cruise tourists and locals.

## In the Tourist Bubble?

One of the main characteristics of cruise tourism, which is relevant for creating spaces for encounters between tourists and locals, is the closeness of the world on the cruise ship. Cruise passengers get everything they need on board: they can choose between several restaurants with different styles, have on-board accommodation, and various offers of entertainment which vary from theatre plays and concerts to dance classes – some cruise ships are even equipped with climbing walls or ice-skating arenas.

Carnival Cruise Line was the first cruise line in the era of mass-market cruise tourism to introduce their cruise ships as "Fun Ships", advertising ships as floating tourist attractions and holiday destinations (Weaver, 2006). Hence, the cruise ship developed from a certain mode of transportation to a tourist attraction itself, wherein a Disneyification of cruise travel can be seen (see Knowledge Box 2).

The design of modern cruise ships follows the main principles of Disneyland Parks (Weaver, 2006). The ships are themed environments with the purpose for passengers to have fun and spend money. A cruise ship can be designed with one ship-wide theme or several themes. Therein, various modes of consumption are connected, e.g., entertainment, merchandise and tourist attractions. The direct linkage of pleasure and profit is a main feature of modern cruise ships. Moreover, emotions are part of the world of profit. Cruise ship employees perform emotional labour as expressing or suppressing particular emotions becomes part of their jobs.

---

**Knowledge Box 2: The Roots of Disneyification**

The first Disneyland Park was opened in Anaheim in California, US, in 1955 and embodied a new concept of amusement parks. The concept of Disneyland Parks differed from the usual amusement parks at this time, which were similar to fairgrounds. In contrast, Disneyland Parks integrated amusement rides in a complete artificial landscape. They were and still are holiday destinations, offering food and accommodation.

Disneyland Parks are characterized by four main principles (Weaver, 2006):

1. They are themed areas with a focus on visual motifs.

2. In most of the cases, the distinction between different types of consumption disappears.

3. The sale of merchandise is promoted.

4. Employees perform emotional labour.

Based on these characteristics, Disneyland Parks are "tourist bubbles". By entering the park, the tourist becomes part of a world, which is separate from the outside world and functioning in itself, being thereby completely artificial. Artificial attractions serve as main sightseeing attractions.

Starting with the first Disneyland Park, a "Disneyization" spread throughout the US and from there worldwide, by which main features and characteristics of Disneyland Parks were adopted in other areas, e.g. restaurants or hotels (Bryman, 1999) and cruise ships.

---

## Shore Excursions

Even though modern cruise ships are tourist destinations themselves, on-shore destinations are still of high relevance for cruise tourism. Going on a cruise includes - in most of the cases - traveling from destination to destination on a planned route. The cruise ship itinerary directs which destinations will be visited, how many days will be spent at sea as well as the length of stay at each destination. The length of stay at a destination differs between cruise lines, but in general cruise ships arrive at a port in the morning and depart in the afternoon (Gibson & Parkman, 2019). Depending on where the cruise port is situated at a destination, the cruise passengers need time to get from the ship to the main sightseeing attractions. Hence, the stay at the destination itself can be even shorter. In regard to cruise passengers' authentic experiences during their shore excursions, Cartwright & Baird state, relating to MacCannell's concept of staged authenticity:

> Given the short length of stays in a port, the cruiser can only, at best, gain an impression of the culture and true nature of a destination. Arranged cultural events and 'folkloric' shows can only accurately be described as staged authenticity. (Cartwright & Baird, 1999, 160)

Cruise passengers can decide if they book shore excursions in advance with the cruise line or if they explore a destination by themselves. Pre-booked tours have the advantage that everything is organized in advance. The moment passengers leave the ship in the morning, busses are already waiting to pick them up in the port. Tour guides accompany the groups and show them all places of interest. The length of the tour is planned and aligned to the cruise ship's schedule. In contrast, people who spend their time at the destination without a pre-booked tour have to organize everything by themselves. This can be less expensive, but also more stressful.

Cruise tourists do not have much time to get to know the culture of the destination they visit. They may have contact to locals such as tourist guides or sellers in shops, but they will not be able to dive deeper into the culture. The description of traditional or stereotypical shore excursions by London (2011) points this out:

> 50 or 60 fellow cruise passengers being ferried around by coach to the scenic and cultural highlights of the port city, stopping for photo opportunities, lunch and a late afternoon visit to the recommended jewellery or craft shop. (London, 2011, 187)

However, there is a trend recognizable that cruise tourists, most of all younger ones, expect shore excursions to be more individual. They should satisfy various interests such as sports, food or wine, and be visually active. But most important, they should be perceived as authentic (London, 2011). Hence, authentic experiences are a main demand of tourists nowadays, even in mass tourism sectors like cruise tourism. From visiting wine yards and trying different wines to watching artisans and participating in their work – an increasing number of tourists want to experience local customs by taking part. They expect shore excursions to go beyond guided tours to sightseeing attractions. Cruise lines react to this demand by offering special shore excursions. These shore excursions are an opportunity to overcome the "tourist bubble" and create spaces for encounters between locals and tourists.

## Creating Spaces for Encounters between Locals and Tourists

Overtourism and cruise tourism seem to hinder encounters between tourists and locals. However, best practice examples show that there are different possibilities to create spaces for these encounters and thereby foster intercultural exchange and understanding.

## Guided Tours by Locals

Individual tours guided by locals are possibilities for tourists to have encounters with locals in times of overtourism. There are various internet platforms such as getyourguide.com,withlocals.com, viator.com, toursbylocals.com or showaround.com where tourists can book local guides. The main advantage is that locals know the place where they live very well. Therefore, they can show different places and guide tourists along different roads to avoid crowded places. Many guides are quite young, sometimes not born in the destination, but living there and familiar with the place. For some platforms, guides make their own prices; for others, prices are fixed and tourists do only choose a guide. Local guides introduce themselves creating individual profiles on these platforms. All these platforms focus on the promise that having local guides automatically would lead to authentic experiences. Spotted by Locals link their offers to ways of how to cope with overtourism:

> In cities where lots of tourists go our locals are looking to make a difference by encouraging travelers to visit spots outside of the touristy city center and discover different authentically local neighborhoods. (Spotted by Locals, 2020)

Individual tours in small groups are good possibilities for tourists to avoid crowded places. Still, first time visitors usually want to see a destination's main sightseeing attractions. However, local guides can try to avoid busy hours or choose different routes to get there. Usually, individual guided tours consist of less people and therefore occupy less space. However, it can be a bigger organizational effort for cruise tourists to take part in these tours than to go on a pre-booked shore excursion with the cruise line.

## Individual Shore Excursions

Most high standard cruise lines offer a wide range of shore excursions, with a focus on more personal and authentic experiences. Also a lot of middle-class cruise lines align their program with tourists' desire for authenticity. Azamara Club Cruises, a Royal Caribbean luxury cruise line with three small cruise ships, launched their program "Cruise Global, Taste Local" in 2015. Locals recommend dining options at their home destination, e.g., Marseilles or Santorini. The recommended restaurants are collected in a guide, which is distributed on-board the ship. Hence, cruise passengers have the possibility to dine like locals (Azamara, 2015). An advantage of the program is that cruise passengers spend their money at local restaurants. But offers like this only work if cruise ships stay a whole day or overnight at a destination. Another program offered by Azamara Club Cruises is the "Cruise Global, Meet Local" shore excursion program. The program directly addresses tourists' demand for authentic experiences. Passengers can visit families at their homes, enjoy local meals with them and listen to their stories about local life, for example in Turkey or the Netherlands. In Montenegro, cruise passengers can visit local families' homes and see their olive oil production, including trying their products. Azamara Club Cruises promotes the program using the following comment of a guest:

> I have been on tours to visit locals in their homes before and in some instances, I have found that they were boring, scripted, and a bit of a dog-and-pony show. Bottom line, my Azamara Cruise Global, Meet Local tour was engaging, entertaining and genuine. (Azamara, 2020)

The excursion is evaluated regarding the degree of perceived authenticity. The guest states that the difference between this tour and previous ones is the fact that this one is "genuine" and "engaging" instead of being "scripted" and presentation-like. Many luxury cruise lines offer these kinds of programs. With AIDA Selection, AIDA Cruises offers a whole program for "fascinating cultures, encounters with locals, fascinating nature and culinaric discoveries", enhancing "authentic travel experiences" (AIDA, 2020; translation by author). The focus is on special routes, regional and seasonal specialities, country-specific culture, a personal atmosphere and longer stays in ports. AIDA introduces locals, who show tourists around the destination, as "Local Heroes", which let the program appear as being even more special.

Other examples of how cruise tourists and local communities can get in contact are programs labelled as "cruise voluntourism" like "You Care, We Care" by Crystal Cruises, "Cruise with Purpose" by Holland America Line or "Give Back with Purpose" by Carnival Cruise Line. Excursions vary from helping to build schools over cleaning beaches to planting trees. Moreover, cruise lines offer excursions where cruise tourists do not help directly with their physical power, but money collected from fees for the excursions goes to local projects or communities. Examples are whale watching excursions in Alaska or visiting traditional communities in Mexico. Cruise lines advertise these excursions by pointing out that they are a possibility for cruise passengers to give something back to local communities. An idea, which aligns with altruistic motifs of tourists who decide to volunteer during their holidays (Brown, 2005). Despite the positive motivation of volunteering tourists, volunteering tourism has been criticised in general for bearing the risk of creating dependencies or neglecting local communities' real needs (Guttentag, 2009). Hence, it is important that volunteering programs do not only focus on the tourist experience, but on how local communities can most benefit from the collaboration. In this case, these programs can create spaces for mutual cultural encounters (McIntosh & Zahra, 2007; Raymond & Hall, 2008). In cruise voluntourism programs, cruise passengers' time for their volunteering experience is limited. Therefore, these excursions have to be well-structured to create the biggest possible positive effect for local communities as well as for tourists themselves.

Cruise voluntourism is still a travel niche. By now, most cruise passengers choose traditional shore excursions or excursions, which involve tasting local products. Even though most cruise passengers leave the ship to explore a destination, there are always some passengers, who stay on board while the ship is in port. A possibility to enable these passengers to get in contact with local culture can be managed by "bringing local products to the ship" (London, 2011, 190). Offers like this can also contribute to an opening of the cruise ship as a tourist bubble.

All these programs show possibilities to cope with overtourism as they enable cruise passengers to visit other places than sightseeing attractions at a destination. Hence, it reduces pressure on crowded places in a destination. Furthermore, tourists contribute to the local community, either by doing physical work or by spending money. Such an engagement can foster better understanding between tourists and locals.

## Conclusion

The cruise tourism market is growing worldwide. While on the cruise ship, passengers stay in a "tourist bubble", they also stay in the tourist bubble when they take part in classical shore excursions. As cruise tourism is often addressed in the context of overtourism, locals can have prejudices against cruise tourists. An increasing number of destinations is effected by overtourism. Overtourism can create tensions between tourists and locals as the impact of tourism is perceived negative by locals. The creation of spaces, in which an encounter between tourists and locals can take place, can foster intercultural exchange between these two groups and reduce tensions. Therefore, cruise lines and travel agencies can take advantage of the fact that most tourists are looking for authentic experiences. Tours that focus on authentic experiences can create spaces for encounters between tourists and locals. Even though these experiences are staged and therefore not purely authentic, they are valuable opportunities. Several cruise lines respond to the growing expectation of cruise passengers for authentic experiences and offer corresponding excursions. Excursions of this type can involve visiting local artisans or wine yards, taking part in workshops and tastings or volunteering in local community projects. For cruise passengers, who do not want to take part in pre-booked shore excursions as well as for daily visitors, individual guided tours by locals are good alternatives to avoid crowded places and busy times. Hence, all these tours create spaces, where tourists can get in contact with locals, and therefore foster intercultural exchange. Furthermore, they contribute to coping with some of the problems of overtourism by helping to spread tourists and reduce pressure on sightseeing attractions at destinations.

The recent COVID-19 pandemic has a huge impact on the tourism sector as traveling for pleasure is not possible in most parts of the world due to various reglementations. It is likely that the COVID-19 pandemic will also affect the tourism sector in the future. In the cruise sector, outbreaks of illnesses, e.g., norovirus, have been well-known problems even before the COVID-19 pandemic (Klein & Lück & Poulston, 2017). Due to the relatively high number of people using the same facilities and the limited space on board a cruise ship, illnesses can spread rapidly and become a serious issue. In the recent COVID-19 pandemic, several cruise ships have been affected either by cruise passengers and crew being trapped on board due to COVID-19 infections or by destinations prohibiting disembarkation. Even though the heightened risk of a rapid spreading of illnesses on cruise ships has been a topic before, the intensity and number of ships affected by COVID-19 could make tourists more aware of health risks connected to cruise travel. The cruise industry will have to come up with new and well-elaborated health safety concepts to maintain passengers' trust.

## Five Major Takeaways

1. Tourism enables encounters between tourists and locals. Therefore, tourism is important as it fosters intercultural communication and exchange.

2. The majority of tourists expects to have authentic experiences during their holidays.

3. Overtourism and the negative perception of cruise tourists can lead to tensions between locals and tourists.

4. Small, individual guided tours by locals are good possibilities to avoid crowds. Shore excursions with a focus on volunteering or alternatives to typical sightseeing tours are good opportunities for tourists to experience destinations offside classical routes.

5. Tours and excursions, which focus on authentic experiences, are valuable in creating spaces for encounters between tourists and locals.

# REFERENCES

AIDA (2020). AIDA Selection. Retrieved from https://www.aidaselection.de

Azamara (2020). Insider Access. Retrieved from https://www.azamara.com/fi/blog/insider-access-kusadasi-turkey

Azamara (2015). Cruise Global, Taste Local. Retrieved from https://www.azamara.com/fi/loyalty/news/azamara-club-cruises-announces-cruise-global-taste-local

Brown, Sally (2005). Travelling with a purpose: understanding the motives and benefits of volunteer vacationers. *Current Issues in Tourism*, 8(6), 479-496.

Bryman, Alan (1999). The Disneyization of Society. *The Sociological Review*, 47 (1), 25-47.

Cartwright, Roger, Baird, Carolyn. 1999. *The Development and the Growth of the Cruise Industry*. Oxford: Butterworth-Heinemann.

CCL (2020). Mardi Gras. Retrieved from https://www.carnivalcruiseline.de/de/mardi-gras

CLIA (2020). Cruise Lines International Association (CLIA) Releases 2021 State of the Cruise Industry Outlook Report. Retrieved from https://cruising.org/en-gb/news-and-research/press-room/2020/december/clia-releases-2021-state-of-the-cruise-industry-outlook-report

CLIA (2018). *State of the Cruise Industry Outlook*. Retrieved from https://cruising.org/news-and-research/research/2018/december/2018-clia-state-of-the-industry

D'Eramo, Marco (2018). *Die Welt im* Selfie – *Die Besichtigung eines touristischen Zeitalters*. Berlin: Suhrkamp.

Dowling, Ross, Weeden, Clare (2017): The World of Cruising. In: ibid. (eds.). *Cruise Ship Tourism*. 2nd Ed. Oxfordshire: CABI, 1-40.

Gibson, Philip, Parkman, Richard (2019). *Cruise Operations Management: Hospitality Perspectives*, 3. Ed. Oxon/New York: Routledge.

Guttentag, Daniel A. (2009). The Possible Negative Impacts of Volunteer Tourism. In: *International Journal of Tourism Research*, 11(6), 537-551.

Jack, Gavin, Phipps, Alison (2005): Tourism and Intercultural Exchange – Why Tourism Matters. In: *Tourism and Cultural Change*, 4, Sheffield Hallam University, UK: Centre for Tourism and Cultural Change.

Klein, Ross, Lück, Michael, Poulston, Jill (2017). Passengers and risk: Health, Wellbeing and Liability. In: Dowling, Ross, Weeden, Clare (eds.). *Cruise Ship Tourism*. 2nd Ed. Oxfordshire: CABI, 106-123.

London, Wendy (2011). Shore-side Activities. In: Vogel, Michael, Papathanassis, Alexis, Wolber, Ben (eds.): *The Business and Management of Ocean Cruises*, Oxfordshire: CABI, 184-195.

Lowry, Richard S. 1991. Framing the Authentic: The Modern Tourist and The Innocents Abroad. *New Orleans Review*, 18 (2), 18-28.

MacCannell, Dean (1976). *The Tourist. A new Theory of the Leisure Class*. Berkley/Los Angeles/London: University Press.

McIntosh, Alison J., Zahra, Anne (2007). A Cultural Encounter through Volunteer Tourism: Towards the Ideals of Sustainable Tourism? In: *Journal of Sustainable Tourism*, 15(5), 541-556.

Morgan, Patsy, Power, Lisa (2011): Cruise Tourism and the Cruise Industry. In: Robinson, Peter, Heltmann, Sine, Dieke, Peter (eds.): *Research Themes for Tourism*. Oxfordshire: CABI, 276-288.

Ponton, Douglas M., Asero, Vincenzo (2018): Representing Global Cruise Tourism: A Paradox of Sustainability. In: *Critical Approaches to Discourse Analysis across Disciplines*, 10 (1), 45-62.

Raymond, Elize M., Hall, Colin M. (2008). The Development of Cross-cultural (Mis)Understanding through Volunteer Tourism. In: *Journal of Sustainable Tourism*, 16(5), 530-543.

Spotted by Locals (2020). What we do to help combat overtourism.
    Retrieved from
    https://www.spottedbylocals.com/blog/overtourism/

Twain, Mark. (1896, reprint 2010). *The Innocents Abroad.* Hertfordshire: Wordsworth Classics.

UNWTO (2020). *World Tourism Barometer*, 18 (1). Madrid: UNWTO.

UNWTO (2018). *'Overtourism'? – Understanding and Managing Urban Tourism Growth beyond Perceptions.* Madrid: UNWTO.

Weaver, Adam (2006). The Disneyization of Cruise Travel. In: Dowling, Ross, Weeden, Clare (eds.). *Cruise Ship Tourism.* 2nd Ed. Oxfordshire: CABI, 389-396.

Chapter 2

# Community Conservancies in Africa Enhance Wildlife Conservation, Community Livelihoods and Cultural Tourism

*Kathleen H. Fitzgerald*

> *Ultimately conservation is about people. If you don't have sustainable development around these parks, then the people will have no interest in them, and the parks will not survive.*

> – Nelson Mandela (*Equilibrium Research*, 2019).

## Introduction

Jocelyn is one of the only female guides in the famous Maasai Mara National Reserve in southern Kenya. With over 150 lodges in the Mara landscape, not including the Serengeti National Park, which borders the Mara Reserve on the Tanzania side, and more than 150,000 tourists (Institute for Economic Affairs, 2016) visiting on an annual basis, one might expect to find more female guides. However, over the course of the three days with Jocelyn, we learn about the cultural barriers for Maasai girls to obtain higher education and professional training. We hear about families ostracizing those who go against cultural norms. Our visit to the Mara is a blend of exceptional wildlife viewing and cultural exploration. We traverse the mesmerizing savannah landscape, watch lions eat a buffalo kill, wait as a leopard emerges from a rocky outcrop and observe a herd of elephants splashing in a muddy pool. We visit a traditional Maasai boma (homestead) and over chai (Kenya tea), on game drives and back at camp around the fire we learn from Jocelyn about Maasai culture.

David is a Bushman from the Central Kalahari Game Reserve in central Botswana. He is a small man with a big smile. He is twenty-five years old and works at a tourism lodge in the Reserve that hires mostly Bushmen and women from the local community. David speaks openly about the importance of the Bushmen culture to him and his simultaneous thirst for an education, money and the opportunity to live in a contemporary house and partake in what people refer to as the modern world. He explains how the elders in his village who still live traditionally as hunter and gatherers support his employment at the lodge despite this being profoundly different from anything they have ever experienced. David recognizes the challenge and complexity in maintaining the Bushmen traditions while enhancing their well-being as Botswana develops.

In each of these instances my visit is enriched by the direct interaction with individuals from the local community and exposure to their culture. Having the opportunity to learn directly from the guides gives me a unique opportunity to gain knowledge about their traditions and way of life. Both visits are interlaced with planned cultural experiences, such as watching a Maasai dance, visiting Maasai and Bushman villages and going on a mock hunt with the Bushmen to see how they hunt and collect food from the natural environment. These experiences are deepened by having the opportunity to ask questions to Jocelyn and David before, during or after the experience. This helps to avoid stereotypes and misperceptions. In both instances, meals are shared with the guides as well as other local staff, providing another perspective and opportunity, should one desire, to learn more about their culture.

The tourism industry, in both examples, fostered a positive intercultural experience for the visitor. It was not forced, nor was it over-commercialized. It created an enabling environment for the guests to experience and see cultural aspects while enhancing the visit with direct knowledge and interaction from community members. Both places are wildlife destinations, which is the draw for tourists, but the cultural experience greatly enhances the tourism experience. It is very common to hear a tourist who has visited Africa say, 'I came for the wildlife, but was not expecting to be blown away by the people.' As a result of these blended experiences throughout Africa, many tourists, in particular return visitors, seek a trip that combines wildlife and cultural tourism. If designed properly, cultural tourism experiences that are linked to a wildlife product can extend the length of stay for tourists, enhance the tourism product, directly benefit the local cultures and communities, and provide a meaningful cross-cultural experience that cultivates awareness about local cultures.

Tourism is a significant contributor to the economy in parts of Africa and wildlife is the driver of this economic engine, it is one of the primary reasons people visit Africa. The wildlife watching tourism industry provides a ready market for cultural tourism. Combining wildlife and cultural tourism enhances the guest experience and, if structured properly, can support conservation and communities. This chapter explores how the increasing number of community and indigenous conservation areas across the continent enable authentic engagement with local community members and their cultures and can help alleviate the threats to Africa's wildlife and conservation areas and support community development and cultural heritage.

## Africa's Growing Tourism Industry

Tourism is the second-largest generator of Foreign Direct Investment globally, attracting $US 807 B, 4.4% of total investment, in 2016 (Space for Giants, 2019).

Worldwide, the industry's contribution to Global Development Product (GDP) has increased over the past decade and is expected to continue to resume its growth post-COVID-19. Africa is one of the world's fastest-growing regions for travel and tourism (Space for Giants, 2019). While the economic importance of tourism in Africa and the continent's share of the worldwide tourism market are relatively small, 5% of global international arrivals and 3% of global international receipts, tourism has been increasing steadily with an average annual growth rate of international tourist arrivals of approximately 6% per year between 2005 and 2013. During that same period, arrivals grew from 35 million in 2005 to 56 million in 2013. (WTO, 2014) The total international tourism receipts for Africa in 2013 reached US$ 34.2 B (WTO, 2014) and currently accounts for approximately 8.5% of Africa's economy (Space for Giants, 2019). Tourism numbers are projected to more than double during the next decade, reaching 134 million international arrivals by 2030 (WTO, 2014). While this forecast was made prior to COVID-19, tourism is still expected to increase post-COVID.

The global adventure tourism market is the fastest growing sector within the tourism industry. Adventure tourism was valued at US$ 586 B in 2018, and is projected to reach US$ 1,627 B in 2026, a 13% increase (Couhan et al., 2019). Africa's diverse terrain and remote locations make it an ideal location for many nature-based adventure sports, adventures and travelers (World Bank, 2014).

Tourism across Africa varies dramatically. For example, East and Southern Africa attract more tourists and contribute more to the GDP than West and Central Africa (World Bank, 2014). Some countries are high performing tourism destinations supporting robust tourism circuits, global brands and diverse products, such as South Africa, Kenya, Rwanda Namibia and Tanzania. Whereas other countries, while they may hold significant potential, lack the enabling conditions for tourism development such as security, ease of access and entry, suitable infrastructure, developed tourism circuits and a visible wildlife product (Space for Giants, 2019).

Tourism in parts of Africa is recognized as an important driver of economic growth in the form of income generation, rural development and employment. For example, in Kenya, 10% of the GDP comes from tourism. Tourism dominates the service sector, 67% of the economy, it is the third largest source of foreign exchange in the country and supports 9% of Kenya's employment (World Bank, 2017). The central role of tourism in the economy is similar in South Africa. In 2018 travel and tourism in South Africa contributed 1.5 million jobs and 425.8 B Rand (US$ 29.8 B) to the economy, representing almost 9% of all economic activity in the country (World Travel & Tourism Council, 2018).

There are approximately 5.3 million direct tourism jobs in Sub-Saharan Africa pre-COVID. Because tourism touches all sectors of the economy—agriculture, transportation, infrastructure—tourism's total direct and indirect impact on employment in Sub-Saharan Africa is 12.8 million jobs. By 2022, the World Travel & Tourism Council predicts 6.8 million direct jobs in tourism and more than 16 million people employed directly and indirectly through tourism in Sub-Saharan Africa (World Bank, 2014).

Jobs and meaningful employment are priorities for African Governments. According to the African Development Bank (ADB), Africa's youth, aged 15-35, is rapidly growing and expected to double to over 830 million by 2050. ADB further reports that the majority of Africa's youth do not have secure economic opportunities. Of Africa's nearly 420 million youth, one-third are unemployed, one-third are tenuously employed, and only one in six is in wage employment. While 10 to 12 million youth enter the workforce each year, only 3.1 million jobs are created, leaving vast numbers of youth unemployed, resulting in poor living conditions, migration, and potential conflict (African Development Bank, 2016). Job creation is recognized by the World Bank as one of the top ten reasons for developing tourism. In addition, development in rural areas, which may not have other suitable employment opportunities, is also recognized as one of the top ten reasons for developing tourism (World Bank, 2014).

## The Central Role of Wildlife Based Tourism in Africa

Wildlife is the major draw for visitors coming to Africa. A United Nations World Tourism Organization (UNWTO) survey completed in 2014 found that wildlife watching tours represent 88% of the total annual revenues of trips to Africa and the 'safari' is the most popular product. The survey found that four out of five tourists coming to Africa came for wildlife viewing (UNWTO, 2014).

A 2014 World Bank report cites wildlife-based safaris as the primary tourism product for East and Southern Africa, noting that the vast diversity of destinations and the high value associated with "big five" game viewing gives these parts of Africa a competitive advantage over other areas of Sub-Saharan Africa and the rest of the world (World Bank, 2014). In South Africa's Kruger National Park, tourists indicated that large carnivores, such as lions, is an incentive for visitors (Equilibrium Research, 2019).

Cultural tourism was ranked as one of the highest activities to couple with nature-based tourism in an assessment completed by the UNWTO. While their definition of cultural tourism includes history, architecture, tribal and village culture, wine tasting and city tours, it represents a demand for experiences beyond wildlife viewing, (UNWTO, 2014) which presents an opportunity for cultural tourism expansion and integration with wildlife viewing safaris. Snyman and Spenceley (2019) note that along with wildlife tourism in conservation areas, there is a growing demand for cultural tourism.

Given Africa's diverse culture and rich traditions in music, art, dress and dance, cultural tourism presents a substantial opportunity for growth. Promotion of cultural tourism in Africa is already prevalent. Senegal promotes its music festivals (World Bank, 2014); Kenya advertises its rich cultures such as Maasai and Kikuyu; and Ethiopia promotes its churches and religious heritage.

While parts of Africa support a strong wildlife-based tourism sector, there is still significant potential for nature-based tourism growth in other parts of the continent, which have not developed wildlife tourism for various reasons. In addition, with the growing demand for cultural tourism, combining this with wildlife tourism will enhance the overall product, catalyze cultural tourism growth and help ensure the long-term sustainability of both products. Cultural tourism products, ranging from dances to crafts, that have not been developed in conjunction with an on-going business and/or a private sector partner have failed in Africa due to lack of marketing, linkage to market, understanding of product niche, business planning, and management capacity. This results in community disappointment and in some cases animosity if an external party, such as a non-profit organization, was involved in helping to set up the product. The linkage of the cultural product to an existing market and/or on-going business, such as a tourism lodge, is the best way to ensure a steady client base, sustainability and a positive outcome for tourists.

There are exceptions in Africa where the majority of tourists visit a country because of their cultural tourism rather than wildlife. For example, in Ethiopia, more than 886,800 tourists visited the country during the 2016-2017 fiscal year. The tourism sector generated over US$ 3.32 B in revenue (Hailemariam, 2017). A majority of the tourists coming to Ethiopia come for cultural tourism—Ethiopia's heritage is steeped with religious history and its churches are globally unique. The Government of Ethiopia is trying to diversify the tourism product by enhancing their protected areas and wildlife product, in an effort to attract wildlife watchers and keep both the wildlife and cultural tourists in country longer by combining the experiences.

**Africa's Protected Areas and Wildlife**

Africa's protected areas are the main tool for wildlife and biodiversity conservation and remain the fundamental building block for conservation (Fitzgerald, 2015). The continent's expansive and diverse protected area network supports extraordinary wildlife found nowhere else in the world. The viability of the tourism industry hinges on the long-term protection of Africa's natural assets—its wildlife and wild lands. Therefore, if Africa's tourism business is going to be sustained and better yet grow in the future, African governments and partners must ensure the long-term viability and sustainability of its wildlife and protected areas.

The International Union for the Conservation of Nature (IUCN) defines a protected area as (IUCN, 2008) 'An area of land and/or sea especially dedicated to the protection and maintenance of biological diversity, and of natural and associated cultural resources, and managed through legal or other effective means.' IUCN further classifies protected areas into six categories, ranging from Category I, a strict nature reserve/wilderness protection area managed mainly for science or wilderness protection, to Category VI, a Managed Resource Protected Area: protected area managed mainly for the sustainable use of natural resources (IUCN, 2008).

Africa currently supports approximately 8,555 protected areas (Protected Planet, 2020), covering approximately 4.3 million km², 13.8% of the continent's land area. (Space for Giants, 2019). Protected areas secure a diversity of ecosystems, habitat for wildlife and vital ecosystem services upon which wildlife and people depend (Fitzgerald, 2015). However, Africa's wildlife and wildlands are facing severe threats that put its biological diversity and tourism industry at risk.

The United Nations (UN) released one of the most comprehensive assessments on biodiversity in May 2019. They found that nature is declining globally at rates unprecedented in human history. The report concluded that the rate of species extinctions is accelerating, with grave impacts on people around the world, and one million animal and plant species are now threatened with extinction, many within decades, more than ever before in human history (IPBES, 2019).

Africa's wildlife and protected areas face similar trends and are threatened by a number of key threats: poaching, habitat conversion and climate change. Poaching and illicit trade of wildlife products, wildlife crime, has dramatically increased since 2005, endangering some of Africa's most iconic species, such as elephants and rhinos. For example, in South Africa in 2007, 13 rhinos were poached, by 2010 this increased to 333—26 times the amount just three years prior, and by 2014, this increased 90-times to 1,215 known rhinos poached. More than 1,000 rhinos were poached each year between 2013-2018, an unsustainable trend (Save the Rhino, 2020).

Lion (*Panthera leo*), for example, have disappeared from 92% of their historical range, declining from approximately 200,000 a hundred years ago to an estimated 20,000 – 30,000 today (Equilibrium Research, 2019).

Wildlife is also threatened by increasing habitat loss (UNWTO, 2014), which is driven by population growth, unplanned development and agricultural expansion, and resource extraction. Climate change is another primary driver of biodiversity loss and is already altering every part of nature (IPBES, 2019). According to the Convention for Biological Diversity (2018), climate change is likely to become one of the most significant drivers of biodiversity loss globally by the end of the century. In addition, the loss of biodiversity contributes to and accelerates the impacts of climate change—a dangerous, positive feedback loop. For example, deforestation and habitat loss results in carbon dioxide emission, the primary greenhouse gas contributing to climate change (IPBES, 2019).

At the 2015 UN climate change conference in Paris, France, the role of healthy ecosystems was recognized as a major mitigation measure for climate change (World Bank, 2018). Forests and intact ecosystems sequester carbon dioxide; therefore, in addition to reducing carbon dioxide, protecting and restoring natural landscapes is recognized as one of the best ways to reduce the impacts of climate change.

One of the underlying drivers of the threats to wildlife and protected areas in Africa is the lack of engagement of local communities. Communities that live with wildlife shoulder the cost. They lose livestock to predation, bear the cost of crop destruction due to wildlife trampling and/or crop raiding, and suffer injury and death from wildlife. It is widely recognized that if communities do not benefit from wildlife or are not involved in conservation through governance or management, they will not support conservation and may even engage in wildlife crime and other unsustainable land uses. The creation of community and indigenous conservation areas throughout parts of Africa has helped to effectively engage communities and enhance wildlife and habitat conservation. These areas are also ripe for cultural tourism and cross-cultural experiences, which in turn will help generate revenue to support these conservation areas.

## Community Conservation and Cultural Tourism

Despite the number of protected areas, wildlife populations continue to decline at an alarming rate across Africa due the threats highlighted prior and because the protected areas are to small and not connected. As a result, protected areas are not able to support natural processes, wildlife movement and viable populations of certain species (Fitzgerald, 2015). In Kenya for example, approximately 70% of the wildlife live outside of Government protected areas (Sindiga, 1995) There are similar trends in other parts of Africa, causing human wildlife conflict and animosity by communities towards conservation. Consequently, over the past fifteen years, the number of community and privately owned 'conservancies'—a clearly defined area set aside for conservation purposes by communities and/or private landowners—has increased (Fitzgerald, 2015).

In Kenya, for example, there are over 160 conservancies, protecting approximately 6.5 million hectares (KWCA, 2020). These conservancies provide multiple benefits to local people including employment, security, revenue, access to social services and infrastructure. Because these conservation areas are owned by the communities, they have a vested interest in the protection of wildlife and the ecosystem. Conservancies directly impact the lives of 700,000 people in Kenya and protect 65% of the wildlife outside of Government run protected areas. These conservancies support more than 140 tourism facilities (KWCA, 2020), some of which are owned by the local communities and a majority staffed by local community members, from senior to junior positions. The rangers patrolling the conservancies are from the local community, which provides employment and training.

In the Maasai Mara, southern Kenya, there are 15 community conservancies covering an area of 347,011 acres. Thirty-nine tourism partners operate in the conservancies and approximately 14,528 landowners earn more than US$ 4 million annually from tourism. The conservancies employ 280 community rangers (MMWCA, 2019).

The majority of Kenya's wildlife conservancies are located in arid and semi-arid landscapes, home to pastoralists such as the Maasai, Samburu, and Pokot. The identity of these cultures is inextricably linked to their land. For example, the pastoralist culture revolves around livestock, which rely on healthy rangelands for grazing. Conservancies help communities sustain their culture by maintaining open space, which supports the pastoralists way of life. East Africa is unique to other parts of

Africa in that it does not separate livestock from wildlife, except for some areas fenced for rhino, it is a relatively open system. Pastoralist cultures will not survive without vast open grasslands for cattle grazing. While many conservancies have been established for ecological reasons, the cultural benefit is substantial.

Namibia also supports an expansive network of community conservancies. As of 2018, there were approximately 86 registered conservancies in Namibia, covering 166,179 km$^2$, and involving approximately 9% of the Namibian population. The Namibia Association of Community Based Natural Resource Management Organizations (NACSO) defines communal conservancies as: self-governing, democratic entities, run by their members, with fixed boundaries that are agreed with adjacent conservancies, communities or land owner (NACSO, 2020). During 2017, Namibia's 83 community conservancies generated over N\$ 132 M (US\$ 9.2 M) in returns for local communities and supported 5,350 jobs. Sixty-two conservancies hosted a total of 171 enterprises based on natural resources, which generated revenue and employment as well as other spin-off businesses (MET & NACSO, 2020).

Given communities have certain rights over land that comprise conservancies and wildlife, which varies from country to country, they are legitimate partners in conservation and tourism operations. Decentralization of rights over natural resources empowers communities to enter into joint-ventures (JVs) with private sector operators for tourism operations and other conservation enterprises.

In Kenya, financial benefits from conservancies flow directly to the communities and local communities can enter into agreements with private sector partners. In some parts of Kenya, revenue from JVs goes to households via electronic payment to bank accounts, cutting out elite capture and corruption. The businesses that operate in conservancies are staffed by members of the local community, which provides meaningful training and skills development in addition to steady salaries. Tourism in community conservancies is playing a key role in increasing community resilience, diversifying revenue and reducing poverty.

For example, in the Amboseli landscape of southern Kenya, the African Wildlife Foundation (AWF), a not-for profit conservation organization headquartered in Nairobi, Kenya (AWF, 2020), worked with the local Maasai community, the Elerai community, to develop a community owned lodge called Satao Elerai and a wildlife conservancy. The lodge is located on the Elerai community land and managed by a private sector tourism partner, Southern Cross Safaris (Satao Elerai, 2020) The lodge was developed by grant funding, raised by AWF on behalf of the community, and private sector capital from Southern Cross Safaris. The land, owned by the community, was set aside as a wildlife conservancy, in exchange for financial benefits from the tourism facility. The Elerai community leased out the lodge to Southern Cross Safaris for management for 15 years and receives: a lease fee, a conservation fee and a percentage of gross revenue. The contract requires Southern Cross Safaris to hire 85% of the staff from the local community. Including wages, the community generates approximately US\$ 230,000 per annum, as of 2017 (Snyman, S & Spenceley, A., 2019). The community are legitimate partners in this JV and have a vested interest in its success, therefore are motivated to protect the wildlife and the conservancy upon which the tourism product depends.

Elerai conservancy was part of an assessment on land use change in Kenya. Using a satellite image time series, researchers recorded threat-based development anthropogenic modification of natural areas and the density of structures for community conservation areas and conservancies. They found that community conservancies with tourism lodges were more effective at controlling development than those without a lodge, particularly in the conservation zones and, to a lesser degree, in the grazing zones (Williams, D. Sumba, D. Muruthi, P. & Gergory-Michelman, N., 2017). Other studies have demonstrated higher conservation performance in community conservation areas than unprotected community lands. In the case of Amboseli, the engagement of communities around the Park in tourism revenues was demonstrated as a strong contributing factor to an increase in wildlife (Western, D., Russell, S., & Cuthill, I., 2009).

The Elerai community established a cultural village that is linked directly to the lodge. Visitors are given the option to visit the cultural village, which employs approximately 48 women (Snyman, S. & Spenceley, A., 2019). The direct linkage to the lodge means that the cultural village has a relatively steady flow of customers. In addition to the funding generated by the visits, the members of the community sell their crafts directly to visitors at the lodge and cultural village, thereby cutting out any middle traders, and providing a good customer base from the lodge.

Satao Elerai guests are also given the opportunity to walk with Maasai on field walks from the lodge and to take part in other cultural activities such as spear throwing. They can meet the community rangers to gain a greater understanding of wildlife management and anti-poaching. Given the majority of the staff are from the community, guests are constantly interacting with the Maasai and given the opportunity to learn about the Maasai culture from observation, participation in activities and discussion. This is radically different than tourists who spend perhaps one hour during their safari learning about 'local culture' through a lecture, film or staged experience.

A key element to ensuring guests take advantage of this opportunity is ensuring they understand the lodge, its history and composition of staff. This is done in a number of ways at Elerai. When guests check in they are given a briefing about the lodge and its history. A plaque on the wall also explains founding partners and information in the room explains the community ownership. The ownership and direct engagement of community members in management is a value addition for tourists and a major draw for visitors who want a cultural and wildlife experience. It differentiates the lodge from the other facilities in the landscape that focus mainly on wildlife and provide a more commercial cultural experience.

Kenya's community conservancies have helped enhance wildlife conservation by increasing land under conservation and involving communities living with wildlife. In addition, community conservancies create an intimate and authentic tourism experience that blends wildlife and cultural tourism. While studies show that visitors come to Kenya come for the wildlife, anecdotal evidence from tourists who stay in community conservancies suggests that visitors are equally enamored by the culture and the people. Given the number of existing and developing conservancies in Africa, there is a significant opportunity to design the tourism product in a way that enables tourists to learn from the communities about the local culture. By improving and diversifying the product, guest will stay longer, which will result in more financial resources for communities and conservation. In addition, this combination provides guests with a better product leading to higher customer satisfaction and return visits.

Conservancies have also helped prevent the erosion of Maasai culture. For example, the Amboseli ecosystem has been occupied by Maasai pastoralists for centuries. The Maasai rely heavily on community lands for grazing livestock, sourcing medicinal plants, building materials and firewood. The community lands, called group ranch lands, around Amboseli National Park were sub-divided into 60- and 10-acre plots over the past ten – fifteen years. These plots are far too small to graze livestock and sustain the traditional Maasai way of life (AWF, 2013). Due to sub-division, the Maasai are gradually losing their most productive land and being pushed into drier areas. This is also resulting in habitat loss and fragmentation of wildlife movement corridors (Kimania & Pickard, 1998).

The sub-division of land is primarily due to: a breakdown in communal systems; failure of the communal system to deliver equitable benefits and improve livelihoods to communities; and socio-economic changes such as a more sedentary way of life, which is in part a response to government policies prescribing a sedentary lifestyle (AWF, 2013). As a result, some of the landowners of the sub-divided parcels worked with local non-profit organizations and formed conservancies, which support wildlife and livestock. There is significant land speculation in the Amboseli landscape and some of the Maasai have sold their land. These land sales have exacerbated poverty as many of the Maasai spend the money fetched from the land sale, have no place to graze their livestock and move to peri-urban or urban areas, such as Nairobi or Mombasa, for employment, which is scant.

## Conservancies Complement State Protected Areas

Community conservancies complement state protected areas ecologically, socially and economically. In 2014, a study was completed in Kenya assessing the complementarity between community conservancies in the Maasai Mara landscape, southern Kenya, and in the Ewaso ecosystem of central Kenya. They found that while most of the conservation areas assessed were created with an ecological focus, the benefits far surpass biological conservation and include social, economic and capacity benefits. The assessment concluded that total environmental outcomes of each protected area network are better for having a mix of state, private and community conservation areas (AFD, 2014). Put simply, the whole is better than the part.

Figure 1: The benefits of community conservancies and indigenous conservation areas in Africa.

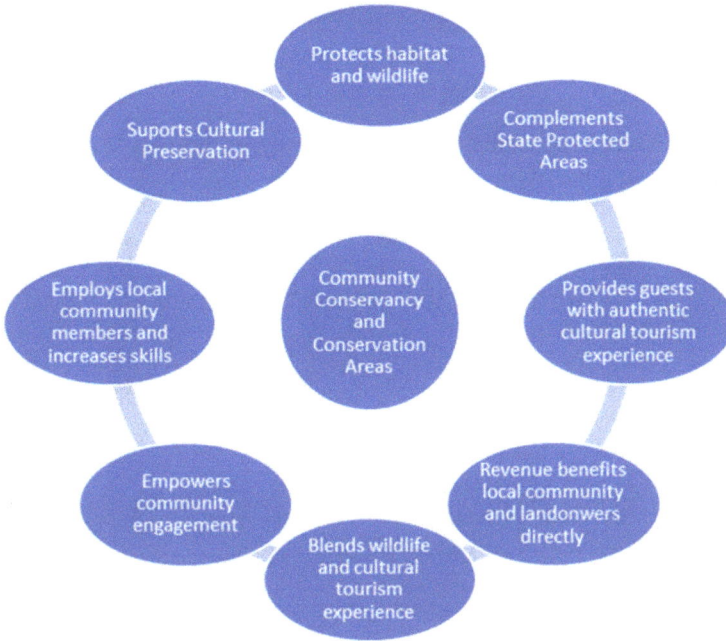

Source: Author

Community conservancies offer a different tourism experience than national parks, especially cultural exposure and interaction. In addition, tourists can partake in activities in conservancies such as walking, mountain biking, riding horses or camels and night game drives, which are not often allowed in national parks. There is a growing demand for these kind of experiences in particular with return visitors to Africa who do not want to sit in vehicles for the duration of their safari. However, tourists are more familiar with national parks than conservancies; therefore, the parks are the anchor and draw for tourists.

For example, the Maasai Mara National Reserve has name recognition because of the wildebeest migration. The adjacent Naboisho Conservancy, which provides a similarly spectacular wildlife experience, is not as well known. Therefore, combining the two is a way to attract visitors to the landscape and diversify their experience, and ideally extend their length of stay.

## The Opportunity for Community Conservancies

Trends indicate that many tourists seek 'green' or 'sustainable' tourism products. These definitions vary, but overall many tourists are looking for ways to ensure their visits support tourism operations that have recycling, water and energy conservation, and contribute positively to wildlife conservation, community development and local production.

The Center for Responsible Travel conducted a number of assessments on consumer behavior and found that more than one third of travelers favor environmental friendly tourism and spending on ecotourism is increasing six times more than the industry rate. Approximately 61% of American tourists feel that travel experiences are better when the destination is a well-preserved natural, historical, or cultural site. Fifty-five percent of travelers want their spending and giving to help the places they visit. Forty-two percent (25 million) of German tourists think that it is particularly important to find environmentally-friendly accommodation and 66% percent of global consumers are willing to pay more for sustainable brands that are committed to social and environmental values (Kenya Tourism Board, 2016). These trends bode well for community conservancies because:

1. Consumer spending in conservancies directly supports the local community and conservation.

2. Community conservancies combine natural and cultural areas.

3. Many of the lodges in community conservancies are sustainably designed and embrace eco-elements such as alternative energy, water conservation and recycling.

4. Community conservancies provide an opportunity for guests to engage directly in social and conservation programs.

Community conservancies, on average, provide a more exclusive experience for tourists. Some of Kenya's most popular protected areas are over-crowded. For example, in the Maasai Mara National Reserve in southern Kenya it is not uncommon for more than thirty vehicles to surround a predator, such a lion or cheetah. This presents a very stressful situation for the wildlife and the tourist. During the wildebeest crossing there may be fifty vehicles along the Mara River waiting to watch a wildebeest crossing. Some conservancies regulate visitation. For example, the Naboisho Conservancy, north of the Maasai Mara, owned by Maasai landowners, regulate the number of vehicles per animal. Only two vehicles, for example, can park next to a lion for wildlife watching. This appeals to tourists who are willing to pay more for a more exclusive experience. Studies show that Asian travelers are more sensitive to overcrowded places than European or American travelers (Northflash

Sustainable Destination Services-Consultancy, 2018). Given the increase in Asian tourists in Africa, this provides a competitive advantage to community conservancies.

## COVID-19

COVID-19 has had a cataclysmic impact on the tourism industry in Africa, community conservancies and state protected areas across Africa. The industry virtually shut down over night (Fitzgerald, 2020). This has resulted in significant job loss for local communities as well as a reduction in revenue from tourism facilities and concession / lease fees from tourism operators to communities and protected area managers. While the pandemic is devastating and at the time this book is going to print, we are uncertain of how and when business will resume, it will resume.

What this means for the African tourism industry is uncertain, however, initial data indicates that smaller tourism facilities will be more attractive to tourists because they are less crowded, volume tourism will take a long time to recover, if at all, depending on health and sanitization rules and regulations, and younger travelers will engage in long-haul travel faster than older more vulnerable populations. In addition, indications from trends in China suggest travelers are interested in outdoor destinations (McKinsey, 2020). This preliminary data bodes well for community conservancies because they offer a more private and exclusive experience. In addition, conservancies appeal to travelers who want to get off the beaten path—these are generally younger travelers who, it is speculated, will be the first to resume long-haul travel.

In Kenya there is discussion about how to resume, restore and re-define Kenya's tourism product post-COVID (Cook, D. & Klassen, G., 2020). Given the ecological, social and economic importance of community conservancies, their ability to provide a blended wildlife and cultural experience, and their draw for the post-COVID traveler community, conservancies should be central to Kenya's marketing and re-defining.

## Conclusion

Africa supports a robust tourism industry that serves as an economic driver in many parts of the continent providing jobs, revenue and contributing to the GDP. While this has been severely stymied by COVID-19, the industry will come back, albeit, potentially different than before. Africa's unique wildlife and wildlands are core to the long-term viability of the tourism industry. There is growing demand for cultural tourism in Africa, in particular as an addition to wildlife safaris. Africa's wildlife is threatened and declining at an unprecedented rate. One of the underlying drivers of this loss is the lack of community engagement. Community conservation areas are increasing across East and Southern Africa and directly engage rural communities in conservation. They protect habitat and wildlife, provide benefits to communities and protect cultural heritage. Community conservancies offer a blend of wildlife and cultural experiences, which is a product that is growing in demand by tourists. By supporting the growth and sustainability of community conservancies, conservation outcomes will be achieved, and social benefits provided to the landowners and local communities. In addition, the blended wildlife and cultural product will enhance the tourist experience and attract visitors and educate tourists about Africa's unique traditions and cultures.

***

A member of a community conservancy in Amboseli invites us to a ceremony called Enkang e-kule, the milk ceremony. Maasai warriors to this date have not eaten any meals with their wives or in front of their mothers. On this day, their mother shaves their head, the warriors paint it red and they prepare to eat for the first time with their wives. We drive a short distance from the community conservancy, across the dry plains to the ceremony site, passing giraffe and zebra on route. When we arrive, I see a sea of red—Maasai in all directions.

Goat is being cooked in a central area. The warriors are in one line and their wives in another. They are smiling, chatting and anxious. When they are called by an elder, they enter a small wood and dung hut together. Inside the wife feeds the Maasai warrior a piece of meat, he then feeds his wife a piece of meat and then she feeds him another piece. This signifies his 'graduation' to being a junior elder. They exit the hut with large smiles. Over 150 men participate in the ceremony.

Once they have all completed the meat-eating ritual, they make two lines, male and female. It sounds like wind chimes from their elaborate beaded and metal jewelry clanging as they walk and stand in the breeze. The wazee, the old Maasai, wait at the entrance and smear goat fat onto the Maasai's heads as they enter as a blessing. They all kneel, and the elders say a prayer. The elders walk through the kneeling group and spray them with milk from a smoked traditional gourd as a final blessing, after which there is more song and dance.

This ceremony is taking place approximately 210 kilometers from Nairobi, a bustling, urban city of five million people. A paved tarmac road runs the entire route with a high-speed train racing alongside the trucks and vehicles. And yet, here, in this savannah woodland the Maasai celebrate a cultural tradition that dates back centuries. They choose to hold onto their culture and to celebrate their heritage. Many of the participants in this ceremony are landowners and members of conservancies that have helped to secure their land, their culture and their way of life.

## Key Takeaways

Africa supports a diverse and robust tourism industry which drives 8.5% of Africa's economy and provides approximately 12.8 million jobs. The primary attraction for visitors to Africa is wildlife; thus, to sustain the tourism industry, Africa's wildlife and wild lands must be protected.

There is an opportunity to expand and diversify Africa's tourism product by combining cultural and wildlife-based tourism, which would help attract tourists, keep them in particular destinations longer and cultivate an awareness and appreciation for Africa's extraordinary cultural diversity and richness.

Wildlife populations are declining in Africa and one of the underlying drivers of the threat to wildlife and habitat protection is the lack of adequate engagement of local communities who live with wildlife and bear the cost.

Over the past fifteen years, community conservancies have increased across parts of Africa securing important habitat and wildlife, benefitting community members directly with revenue, employment and other values, helping to maintain cultures and traditional lifestyles, and providing guests with unique cultural tourism experiences in addition to the traditional wildlife product.

While COVID-19 has had a cataclysmic impact on the tourism industry in Africa, the recovery in Africa will favor community conservancies because they provide an outdoor and off the beaten path experience as well as a more exclusive, less crowded product.

# REFERENCES

African Development Bank. (2016). *Jobs for youth in Africa: Catalyzing youth opportunity across Africa.* Retrieved from https://www.afdb.org/fileadmin/uploads/afdb/Images/high_5s/Job_youth_Africa_Job_youth_Africa.pdf.

African Wildlife foundation. (2013). *Community payment for ecosystem services in the Amboseli Ecosystem: Leasing land for livelihoods and wildlife.* Technical Paper Series. Nairobi, Kenya: Fitzgerald, K.

African Wildlife Foundation. (2020). Retrieved from www.awf.org.

Agence Francaise de Developpment (AfD). (2014). Exploring environmental complementarity between types of protected areas in Kenya. Paris, France: Elliott, J, Gibbons, H, King, D, King A, & T Lemenager.

Chouhan, N., Vig, H., & Deshmukh, R. (2019). *Adventure tourism market.* Retrieved from https://www.alliedmarketresearch.com/adventure-tourism-market.

Convention for Biological Diversity. (2018, November). *The efforts to protect and restore habitats not only benefit biodiversity but also offer cost-effective and proven measures to mitigate and adapt to climate change.* Retrieved from https://www.cbd.int/article/biodiversityloss-climatechange.

Cook, D. & Klassen, G. (2020, April). Recovery and renewal for Kenya. Presentation conducted at Kenya Ministry of Tourism post covid-19 Leap Forward webinar.

Equilibrium Research. (2019). The New Lion Economy. *Unlocking the value of lions and their landscapes.* Bristol, UK: Stolton, S. & Dudley, N.

Fitzgerald, K. (2020, March). COVID-19: Let us put emphasis on risk management. The Standard. Retrieved from https://www.standardmedia.co.ke/article/2001366280/covid-19-let-us-put-emphasis-on-risk-management.

Fitzgerald, K. (2015). The silent killer: Habitat loss and the role of African protected areas to conserve biodiversity. In Wuerthner, G., Crist, E. & Butler, T. (Eds.), *Protecting the Wild. Parks and Wilderness, the Foundation for Conservation* (pp. 170-188). Washington, DC: Island Press.

Hailemariam, Z. (2017, October). Ethiopia Expects 30 Billion Dollars Income from Tourism Sector. *The Ethiopian Herald.* Retrieved from https://allafrica.com/stories/201710110636.html .

Institute for Economic Affairs. (2016). Number of visitors to national parks and game reserves, 2011-2015. Retrieved from http://www.ieakenya.or.ke/number_of_the_week/number-of-visitors-to-national-parks-and-game-reserves-2011-2015.

Intergovernmental Science-Policy Platform on Biodiversity and Ecosystem Services (IPBES). (2019). *Global assessment report on biodiversity and ecosystem services of the Intergovernmental Science-Policy Platform on Biodiversity and Ecosystem Services.* Bonn, Germany. E. S. Brondizio, J. Settele, S. Díaz, and H. T. Ngo (Eds).

International Union for the Conservation of Nature (IUCN). (2008). *Defining protected areas: an international conference in Almeria, Spain.* Gland, Switzerland: Dudley, N. & Stolton, S. (Eds).

Kenya Tourism Board. (2016). Sustainable tourism report 2016. Nairobi, Kenya.

Kenya Wildlife Conservancy Association (KWCA). (2020) *Status of conservancies in Kenya.* https://kwcakenya.com/

Kimani, K & Pickard, J. (1998). Recent trends and implications of Group Ranch sub-division and fragmentation in Kajiado District, Kenya. *The Geographical Journal, 164*(2), 202-213.

Maasai Mara Wildlife Conservancies Association (MMWCA). (2019). *State of Mara conservancies report 2019.* Nairobi, Kenya: Sopia, D., Ole Reson, E., & Mwangangi, J. (Eds).

McKinsey & Co. (2020, April). COVID-19: Disrupting tourism as we know it. Presentation conducted at Kenya Ministry of Tourism post covid-19 Leap Forward webinar.

Ministry of Environment and Tourism (MET) & The Namibia Association of Community Based Natural Resource Management Organizations (NACSO). (2020). *The state of community conservation in Namibia annual report.* Windhoek, Namibia.

Northflash Sustainable Destination Services-Consultancy. (2018). Overtourism: Tourists go home. Retrieved from https://northflash.com/overtourism-tourists-go-home/.

Protected Planet. (2020). Retrieved from https://www.protectedplanet.net/search?q=africa&region=Africa.

Satao Elerai. (2020). Satao Elerai welcomes you. Retrieved from http://sataoelerai.com/.

Save the Rhino. (2020). Rhino info: Poaching statistics. Retrieved from https://www.savetherhino.org/rhino-info/poaching-stats/.

Sindiga, I. (1995). Wildlife-based tourism in Kenya: Land use conflicts and government compensation policies over protected areas. *Journal of Tourism Studies.* 6(2), 45-55.

Snyman, S. & Spenceley, A. (2019). *Private sector tourism in conservation areas in Africa.* Boston, MA: Centre for Agriculture and Bioscience International.

Space for Giants. (2019). Building a wildlife economy: Developing nature-based tourism in Africa's state protected areas. Nairobi, Kenya: Conservation Capital, Space for Giants & Vause, J.

The Namibia Association of Community Based Natural Resource Management Organizations (NACSO). (2020) *Registered communal conservancies.* Retrieved from http://www.nacso.org.na/conservancies.

Western, D., Russell, S., & Innes, C. (2009). The Status of Wildlife in Protected Areas Compared to Non-Protected Areas of Kenya. *PLOS (Public Library of Science) One.* 4(7). https://doi.org/10.1371/journal.pone.0006140.

Williams, D., Thorne, J., Sumba, D., Muruthi, P., & Gregory-Michelman, N. (2018). Evaluating outcomes of community-based conservation on Kenyan group ranches with remote sensing. *Environmental Conservation,* 45(2), 173-182.

World Bank. (2014). *Tourism in Africa harnessing tourism for growth and improved livelihoods.* Development Forum Series. Washington, DC: Christie, I., Fernandes, E., Messerli, H. & Twining-Ward, L.

World Bank. (2017). *An Economic Assessment of Kenya. Standing out of the Herd.* Washington, DC: Sanghi, A., Damania, R., Manji, F.N.M. &Mogollon, M.P.

World Bank. (2018, December). *Outcomes from COP 21: Forests as a key climate and development solution.* Retrieved from https://www.worldbank.org/en/news/feature/2015/12/18/outcomes-from-cop21-forests-as-a-key-climate-and-development-solution.

World Tourism Organization (UNWTO). (2014). Towards measuring the economic value of wildlife watching tourism in Africa briefing paper. Madrid, Spain.

World Travel & Tourism Council. (2018). Retrieved from https://wttc.org/en-gb/Research/Economic-Impact.

# Chapter 3

# Factors Constraining the Loyalty of Cultural Travellers to Havana

*Yen E. Lam González*
*University Institute for Tourism and Sustainable Economic*
*Development (Tides), University of Las Palmas de Gran Canaria,*
*Spain*

*Niurka Cruz Sosa*
*Master Plan for the Integral Revitalisation of the Old Havana,*
*Historian's Office of Havana City,*
*Cuba*

*Javier de León*
*University Institute for Tourism and Sustainable Economic*
*Development (Tides), University of Las Palmas de Gran Canaria,*
*Spain*

## Abstract

Since 2014, Havana has become one of the most visited cities in the Caribbean region, receiving more than a half of the annual tourism arrivals in Cuba, which is a clear indicator of the increasing cultural motivations among travellers to visit the country. However, Cuba's tourism strategy is not taking advantage of this positioning, despite the archipelago's need to move away from its image as a traditional *sun and beach* destination. This research aims to analyse factors constraining tourism loyalty to Havana as a cultural destination. For this purpose, 1500 face-to-face surveys were conducted to tourists during their so-called cultural trip. A structural equation model is employed to analyse the relation between dissatisfaction-based evaluations of tourists of the destination (i.e., products and services that negatively affect their cultural experience) on their behavioural and attitudinal loyalty to Havana. The results are useful for destination managers to better understand the areas that require special attention in their attempt to promote tourism loyalty. It also identifies the attributes that are more likely to favour the tourist's cultural experience in the longer term, such as those related with the enhancement of the social, health, or environmental and economic conditions of Havana, thus contributing to a more sustainable development of the cultural destination.

**Keywords:** Cuba, cultural tourism, Havana, loyalty, tourism planning, sustainability, resilience

# Introduction

In Cuba, international tourism has been strengthened since the beginning of the nineties, as a response to the economic problems that the country was facing. To date, the Cuban tourism strategy has been based on the *sun and beach* model, according to its condition of a Caribbean island and the natural potentialities that it possesses. The cultural heritage of the country has been set aside, although its importance is publicly recognised (Kline, Bulla, Rubright, Green & Harris, 2016). The cities, and specially Havana City, with notable cultural resources, were conceived as transit destinations.

The last thirty years of tourism in Cuba have been characterised by a timid growth in the main indicators of income and arrivals (ONE, 2017). There is public recognition of the need to work towards a more competitive industry (Figueras & Pérez Cárdenas, 2015). This, together with the obsolescence of the traditional *sun and beach* tourism model, the increase of international competition, and the change in the preferences of the demand at a global level (López-Guzman et al., 2013; Twining-Ward, 2010), defines the need to implement new strategies for tourism diversification.

In this scenario, a conjectural phenomenon has appeared to generate a notable impact on international tourism in Cuba (Alarcón & Hechavarría, 2016). This is of course, the new controversial diplomatic relations with the United States, after a half century of pacific enmity. It began in 2014 with the US Government's decision to normalise the diplomatic relations with Cuba and to remove travel restrictions for US citizens leading to an increase of more than 36% of tourism arrivals in the country between 2014 and 2017. In this period, the country broke through the milestone of 3 million international arrivals (ONE, 2017). Later, a drastic decline in the number of international tourists came together with the US Government's decision to scale the treaties back (Chávez, Chávez & Cerdan, 2019).

Along with this changing scenario, the cultural motivations among international tourists in Cuba have increased, and Havana, the capital of the country, with its wide variety of cultural values (i.e., the Historic Centre World Heritage Site), has become a leading destination. In recent years the city has received more than 60% of all the international tourists visiting the country and is positioned in the top three of the most visited destinations in the Caribbean region. However, this positioning may be fundamentally affected by the tremendous uncertainty caused by the 2020 outbreak of COVID19 (Gössling, Scott & Hall, 2020). Thus, solid renovation strategies are needed and they should be centred on a cultural tourism that guarantees social, health and environmentally-friendly services and conditions that enhance the cultural experience value.

At the same time, the measuring and understanding of loyalty is an important aspect that can help cultural destinations to survive in the current competitive and unpredictable tourism sector (Akhoondnejad, 2016). Loyal tourists represent not only a stable source of income for destinations, but also act as a channel of information that informally connects networks of friends and other potential travellers. Repeating tourists are also less sensitive to prices, showing a greater willingness to pay, and also the cost of catering for this type of tourist is lower (Lau & McKercher, 2004; Oliver, 1999). Although there is a considerable amount of academic research measuring and exploring the causes and effects of tourist loyalty, the results do not allow building a theory in the context of cultural destinations, due to the particularities of each site, and the discretionary nature of human preferences (Li et al., 2016) towards cultural attractions, which justify academic attention.

In this sense, the research area of this chapter is concerned with the impact that cultural travellers' opinions and evaluations of Havana as a cultural destination have on the repetition of the visit and the intentions to revisit. Thus, this study provides evidence on the destination attributes that negatively affect cultural tourists' loyalty, which can be useful in planning a new development of cultural tourism in Havana and indeed in several cities of the Caribbean region.

The paper is structured as follows: The next two sections outline the study of cultural tourism and tourist loyalty, with special attention to empirical studies, which have been undertaken in coastal regions and islands -with reference to Cuba-, as well as to the role of destination attributes that may be relevant in explaining the behaviour of cultural tourists. The fourth section describes the evolution of tourism in Cuba and Havana as a cultural destination. The fifth section describes the study; the model and variables used and their measurement. It also presents the fieldwork, the research instrument utilised for data collection and the sample construction. The next section is dedicated to the results of the study, and finally, the last sections are dedicated to the conclusions of the research and the references.

> *The present research identifies those features of Havana that negatively affect cultural tourists' experience and loyalty, which can be useful in planning the development of cultural tourism in several cities of the Caribbean region.*

## Valuing Culture for Sustainable Tourism Development

As Norval (1936) expressed, the history of travel begins in the most remote antiquity and its origins start with human needs. On the other hand, cultural heritage is a witness of the values and work of people, is unique in a physical space and its authenticity turns it into a potential tourism resource able to trigger trips and generate activity at the destinations (McIntosh & Prentice, 1999). Thus, cultural heritage becomes a differentiation key for destinations and takes advantage of the interest generated by its attractions in order to support its rehabilitation and maintain its values (McKercher et al. 2002; Toselli, 2003).

Defining cultural tourism still poses a major debate in literature because the notions of culture, heritage and tourism themselves are so diverse and open to differing interpretations (Richards, 2018). The World Tourism Organization (UNWTO) fails to specify a unique concept of cultural tourism, and emits two technical definitions; a reduced definition which defines it as the movement of people mainly caused by cultural motivations such as study tours, festivals and other artistic events, visits to sites and monuments, study nature, art, folklore and pilgrimages, etc. On the other hand, a more general definition, which defines it as the movement of people seeking to satisfy the human need of diversity, aimed at raising the cultural level of the individuals, providing new knowledge, experiences and encounters (UNWTO, 1995).

On the other hand, ICOMOS, the International Scientific Committee on Cultural Tourism (founded in 1976), defines cultural tourism as that form of tourism whose main purpose is gaining knowledge of monuments as well as historical and artistic sites, and contributes to their maintenance and generates socio-cultural and economic benefits for the local people (Icomos, 1964,1976,1999). By assuming these principles, a large group of travellers and cultural destinations are excluded (Pedersen, 2005).

Meanwhile, Bonink (1992) states that there are two fundamental approaches to the conceptualisation of cultural tourism; a general one, oriented to attractions, and another based on the visitor's experience, motivations and perceptions. The first approach distinguishes cultural tourism as the movements of people to specific cultural attractions, such as heritage sites, artistic and cultural events, art and performances. The second refers to the temporary movement of people into any cultural attraction with the intention of obtaining new information and experiences to satisfy their cultural needs.

In this regard, MacDonald (2004) and Richards (1996, 2011) agree that the main difficulty of the first approach is that it refers to the so-called "high culture", while the current preferences of tourists point towards the diversity of attractions (ordinary consumer of culture). This indicates the complex nature of the cultural tourism subject, which requires multi-disciplinary and multidimensional approaches to capture such complexity (Richards, 2018). Following Richard (2011), this research assumes the first approach, which is believed of great utility for empirical research, especially when it is necessary to identify and quantify the segment (Richards, 2018).

It is estimated that cultural tourism accounts for over 39% of international tourism arrivals (Richards, 2018), with 500 million tourists a year (Jovicic, 2016; Richards, 2011). Strengthening cultural tourism has a positive effect for those destinations with high seasonality (Cisneros-Martínez & Fernández-Morales, 2015), since for this market segment the weather conditions of the destination are not a limiting factor. Cultural tourists spend more and stay longer at the destination on average, thus resulting in a high profitability potential, if compared to other segments

(Csapo,2012). Thanks to its potential, cultural tourism stands out as a key sector for the sustainability of many coastal and island destinations highly dependent on the tourism activity, especially sun and beach tourism products. However, research related to this segment is still considered scarce when compared with the figures of actual and expected economic growth of the activity (Pérez Guilarte, 2014; Smith & Richards, 2013)

Tourists that travel mainly in search of cultural attractions are often called "specific cultural tourists" (Irish Tourist Board, 1988), "culture passionates" (Chias Suriol, 2003) or "culture vultures" (Richards, 2004). This segment tends to book accommodation in hotels or homestays as a second alternative and organise the trip on their own mainly using the Internet (Smith & Richards, 2013; Richards 2011). Literature also recognises that the primary motivation of a cultural traveller is the combination of environment, culture and knowledge, where the search of intangible values and exchanges with residents prevails.

According to studies, the motivations for visiting cultural sites have changed little (Jovicic, 2016; Richards, 2007), although the evolution of ICTs has allowed a greater autonomy in travel planning, without implying a price increase for the intermediation of industry professionals (Richards, 2007). Technological development has also contributed to a change in behavioural patterns in the cultural tourism market. Cultural sites can now be individually consumed thanks to advances in audio-visual technologies (Russo & Van der Borg, 2002). Nowadays, cultural tourists are considered high consumers of ICT, both in the organisation and development of the trip, hence the increasing number of websites and specialised agencies within the sector (Caro, Luque & Zayas Fernández, 2014; Dávid, Remenyik, & Gergely, 2013).

Moreover, authors agree that cultural tourists do not "consume" culture or meet their cultural needs in the same way (Richards, 2007; McKercher, Wong & Lau, 2006), with the socio demographic characteristics of tourists being the main cause of such differences. Preferences and opinions about the cultural attributes of destinations vary among tourists according to their educational level (Correia, Kozak & Ferradeira, 2011), family environment, age (Richards, 2011), lifestyle and social networking (Timothy, 2011) leading to the necessity of the constant updating of research across destinations. From the set of destination attributes that intervene in the conformation of a cultural experience, it has been proven that safety is very important in ensuring market success (Pratt & Tarlow, 2014). Authenticity and hygiene are also found as important components of the cultural experience (Cetin & Bilgihan, 2016), as well as shopping, traffic, noise, transportation, norms and rules, language, chaos, parking, and lack of standards, although they have not been studied in relation to the behaviour of cultural tourists (Cetin & Bilgihan, 2016).

## Tourism Loyalty in the Context of Cultural Destinations

Loyalty has received special attention in tourism marketing literature, because loyal tourists represent not only a stable source of income for destinations, but also act as a channel of information that informally connects networks of friends and other potential travellers (Almeida-Santana & Moreno-Gil, 2018). Repeating tourists are also less sensitive to prices, showing a greater willingness to pay, and also the cost of catering for this type of tourist is lower (Lau & McKercher, 2004; Oliver, 1999).

Tourism loyalty is a construct that has been tackled in a very homogeneous way, but generally adopting three main conceptual approaches: behavioural, attitudinal, and an approach that integrates both attitude and behaviour (Almeida-Santana & Moreno-Gil, 2018; Rundle-Thiele, 2005). In a tourism context, the behavioural approach is most frequently used by researchers, because the final benefits that a loyal tourist brings to a tourist destination are largely motivated by their behaviour (Zhang et al., 2014).

Increasing studies have been dedicated to tourism loyalty, claiming that satisfaction is a major antecedent of loyalty (Ramseook-Munhurrun et al., 2015; Valle, Silva, Mendes & Guerrio, 2006), although several authors have demonstrated that for some specific tourism segments (i.e., cultural tourists), a higher satisfaction level does not necessarily lead to a greater willingness to repeat the visit (Cetin & Bilgihan, 2016).

In addition, research is consistent explaining that the absence of satisfaction (i.e., tourists valuing cultural activities with the lowest rate in a satisfaction scale) does not necessarily mean dissatisfaction (Moreno et al., 2013). The reverse can also occur, where situations can only generate dissatisfaction, whereas their absence does not necessarily lead to satisfaction (Alegre & Garau, 2010). Thus, the analysis of dissatisfaction-based evaluations of tourists can give more accurate results regarding the destinations' inability to promote loyalty, which is considered an under-investigated research area.

In the context of cultural tourism, various researchers have analysed the causes of tourist loyalty, mainly focusing on sports, event and festival market niches (Akhoondnejad, 2016). Research has demonstrated that authenticity, service quality and perceived value are determinants of tourists' loyalty to cultural events (Shen, 2014), but have not been verified to predict loyalty to cultural destinations. Thus, dissatisfaction analysis would help destinations, such as Cuba, to identify the critical areas that need to be improved in order to avoid unsatisfactory cultural experiences affecting a tourist's decision to repeat the visit.

## Origins and Development of Tourism in Cuba

Tourism in Cuba as an economic activity was first developed in the early nineteenth century, associated with the prosperity of the country as a Spanish colony. It is argued that the development of commerce and the arrival of immigrants and foreign visitors to the island generated a demand for housing, which was followed by the appearance of theatres, cafes, dance halls, walkways and parks with music bands, and buildings for cultural and commercial uses (Figueras & Pérez Cárdenas, 2015). In Havana, the capital city, the accommodation and gastronomy services were strengthened because of the existence of the main commercial port of the country (Rodriguez Dominguez, 2002).

In the twentieth century, Cuba being a republic, received an increasing flow of U.S. tourists, mainly for business and leisure purposes. In the thirties, tourism income had become the third largest source of foreign exchange for Cuba, after sugar and tobacco (Figueras & Pérez Cárdenas, 2015). The fifties represented the consolidation of tourism in the country, with an accelerated process of hotel construction. In 1956, 40% of the accommodation capacity of the Caribbean was located in Havana and San Juan of Puerto Rico. The city of Havana witnessed an accelerated process of hotel construction and was positioned as an eminently playful destination, especially oriented to the US market. Havana was hosting 87% of the arrivals to the country (Villalba Garrido, 1993).

Figure 1: Havana foundational city delimitation

*Source: Cruz Sosa, 2009*

In January 1959 with the triumph of the revolution, the scenario of tourism in Cuba was drastically transformed, because of the nationalisation of private enterprises, the closure of casinos and the prohibition of gambling in January 1961. In the early 90's, as a forced response to the country's economic crisis, caused by the fall of the former socialist block, a new tourism development strategy was adopted, which turned tourism once again into a driving force of the national economy. The new national tourism strategy focused on the European and Canadian markets, mainly because mass tourism and the "sun and beach" products were growing in Europe. The strategy considered the cities as transit destinations, giving priority to other coastal areas of the island and to the all-inclusive model. It also contributed to the development of several regions of the country, which are now called *poles* (Chávez et al., 2019). This tourism strategy is publicly considered successful because during the 1990's, it managed to position Cuba among the top ten destinations in Latin America and the second most visited in the Caribbean destination.

In 2010 the number of visitors was seven times higher than the 1990's figure, and gross income had grown by more than eight times, favouring other economic sectors, especially employment. However, in the early nineties, it was forecasted that by 2010 the country would receive approximately 7 million visitors, with revenues of more than 11 000 million dollars (García & Lopez, 2012). In reality, after the historical record of 2005 of 2.3 million visitors, a timid growth was observed in the main tourism indicators in Cuba until 2014, with several relapses (ONE, 2014). The following root causes have been identified: high prices of the supply side, problems concerning the support and service infrastructure, restrictions on travel from the United States, dependence on air transport as the only route, among other circumstances (García & Lopez, 2012) together with the increasing international competition within the tourism industry (Lopez-Guzman et al, 2013).

Cuba crossed the barrier of 3 million tourists in 2014 (for the first time since 1959), a year in which tourism activity contributed to the country's finances by around 2 700 million dollars. This tourism *boom* matches and is probably caused by the occurrence of newly controversial diplomatic relations between Cuba and United States (i.e., Obama's decision to remove travel restrictions for US citizens for the first time since 1959). More recently, tourism arrivals have decreased severely since 2017, which came together with Trump's decision to scale Obama's treaties back (Chávez, Chávez & Cerdan, 2019). Under this changing scenario, Havana, concentrating a great variety of cultural values, tangible and intangible, historical and contemporary, including a World Heritage site: "The Old Havana" (Kline et al.,2016), has recovered its tourism centricity (Chávez et al., 2019). From 2014 to 2018, the city received more than 60% of all the international tourists arriving in the country, with 2.5 million tourists on average (ONE, 2018), gaining a position in the top three of the most visited destinations in the Caribbean region (i.e., Santo Domingo and Puerto Rico received 2.1 and 1.6 million tourists annually for the same period respectively).

Faced with this new scenario, the renewal of the Cuban tourism strategy towards urban-cultural tourism development is crucial (Alarcón & Hechavarría, 2016), thus promoting greater diversification of the supply (Chávez et al., 2019). Havana stands out as an ideal vehicle to foster the development of cultural tourism in Cuba (Perez Guilarte & Echarri Chavez, 2012) and further knowledge of the sector and the market is essential in this process. To this aim, the present research focuses on identifying those attributes that are currently affecting the loyalty of cultural travellers to Havana.

---

*Havana stands out as an emerging urban-cultural destination, and an ideal vehicle to foster the development of cultural tourism in Cuba, but needs to take advantage of new knowledge on the sector and the cultural tourism segment.*

---

## Study Design

In order to assess the relationship between dissatisfaction and loyalty of cultural tourists, various hypotheses were formulated within a model of tourist loyalty with cultural destinations. Thus, the model focused on negative attributes that were evaluated by cultural tourists (DIS), when the purpose of the trip was mainly for visiting cultural attractions and heritage. It also referred to behavioural loyalty as the number of visits made by cultural tourists to the destination (VISIT), and attitudinal loyalty as the intention of tourists to repurchase the cultural destination (REVI).

The starting point was the consideration that the dissatisfaction of cultural tourists with respect to the destination may affect their intentions to repeat the visit in the near future. Also, it was expected that repeating tourists would be those with the lowest levels of dissatisfaction with the cultural city. The hypotheses were studied utilising a system of structural equations, with dissatisfaction (DIS) being a construct grouping negative attributes of the destination, that were rated by tourists using a 7-point Likert scale (1= I totally disagree; 7= I totally agree). Fourteen attributes were identified according to their relevance for the cultural segment and they were grouped in four areas, as shown in table 1.

Table 1: Destination attributes affecting the cultural experience value

| **Tourist facilities and infrastructure**<br>• Lack of professionalism in hospitality services<br>• Facilities and infrastructures in bad conditions<br>• Poor service quality in hotel, restaurants, etc.<br>• Few shopping options | **Transport, signalization and roads**<br>• Car rental/ Taxi unavailable<br>• Bad signposting of roads and/or places of interest<br>• Road in bad conditions<br>• Problems at the airport |
| --- | --- |
| **Hygiene and peace**<br>• Natural environment lacking cleanliness and conservation<br>• Noise<br>• Crowded destination | **Cultural products and services**<br>• Bad promotion of cultural events and programmes locally<br>• Cultural attractions lacking maintenance and conservation<br>• Cultural activities less developed or lacking a business approach |

*Source: Own Elaboration*

The first hypothesis to consider focused on the relevance of the tourist facilities and infrastructures (DIS1) to explain the number of visits (VIST), that is:

Hypothesis 1. Cultural tourists perceiving increased problems with tourist facilities and infrastructure (DIS1) have visited the destination less (VISIT).

Following Cetin & Bilgihan (2016) authenticity, hygiene and the quality of cultural products and services, the transport and roads are important components of the cultural experience; thus, it can be explored if repeating tourists are less unsatisfied with these attributes. Thus, the following three hypotheses of the model were established:

Hypothesis 2. Tourists declaring that the quality of transport, signposting and roads is poor (DIS2) have visited the destination less (VISIT).

Hypothesis 3. Tourists perceiving that the hygiene and environment of the destination is not proper (DIS3) have visited the destination less (VISIT).

Hypothesis 4. Tourists stating that the cultural products and services on offer at the destination are lacking authenticity and proper promotion (DIS4) have visited the destination less (VISIT).

The next group of hypotheses are related to the tourist′s disposition to repurchase the destination (REVI), which is expected to depend on the dissatisfaction with the destination's attributes. Thus, the following four hypotheses of the model were established:

Hypothesis 5. Tourists perceiving more problems with tourist facilities and infrastructure (DIS1) are less willing to re-visit the destination (REVI).

Hypothesis 6. Tourists considering that the quality of transport, signposting and roads is poor (DIS2) are less willing to re-visit the destination (REVI).

Hypothesis 7. Tourists perceiving that the hygiene and environment of the destination is not proper (DIS3) are less willing to re-visit the destination (REVI).

Hypothesis 8. Tourists stating that the cultural products and services on offer at the destination are lacking authenticity and proper promotion (DIS4) are less willing to re-visit the destination (REVI).

It can also be expected that repeating tourists have greater disposition to repurchase the destination. Therefore, the ninth hypothesis is proposed:

Hypothesis 9. Tourists who have visited the destination on more occasions (VISIT) are more willing to re-visit the same destination in the near future (REVI).

Figure 2 depicts the path diagram, considering all the elements described above and the hypotheses presented. The variables REVI (intention to revisit), VISIT (number of visits) were drawn in boxes because they are actual data collected during the fieldwork. The latent variable constructs (DIS1 to DIS4) were displayed as circles or ellipses representing explanatory or exogenous variables. The VISIT and REVI variables are predicted by DIS1 to DIS4 constructs, in that no other variable in this particular model predicts them. Finally, the VISIT variable acts as an endogenous and exogenous variable also explaining REVI. The negative relation between DIS constructs and the variables REVI and VISIT proves the constraining effect of the attributes on tourist loyalty.

Figure 2: Theoretical model

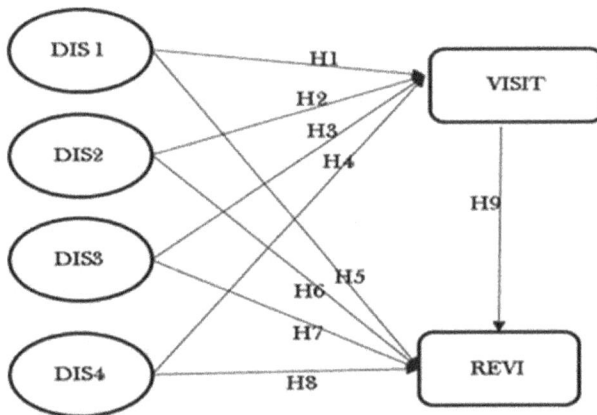

*Source: Own Elaboration*

Mathematically, the model is represented by three structural equations:

1. $VISIT = \gamma 1\ DIS1 + \gamma 2\ DIS2 + \gamma 3\ DIS3 + \gamma 4\ DIS4 + \varepsilon 1,$

2. $REVI = \gamma 5\ DIS1 + \gamma 6\ DIS2 + \gamma 7\ DIS3 + \gamma 8\ DIS4 + \varepsilon 2,$

3. $REVI = \lambda 1\ VISIT + \varepsilon 3,$

Where VISIT and REVI are the endogenous variables of the model, and γ1 to 8 and λ1 are the regression coefficients to be estimated. On the other hand, the exogenous indicators that define the constructs DIS1, DIS2, DIS3 and DIS4 in the measurement model are observed variables corresponding to the fourteen attributes that were rated by tourists (as shown in table 1).

## Data Collection

The target population of the study was defined as tourists visiting Havana motivated by visiting cultural attractions, museums and the heritage of the destination. Previous to the surveying phase, the questionnaire was translated into four languages, and a focus group was conducted with ten cultural tourists of different nationalities, coming from the main outbound markets (Canada, Spain, USA, France). The purpose was to ensure that the questions were going to be clearly understood by the respondents. Once the questionnaire was pre-tested and the pertinent corrections made to the items that raised comprehension difficulties, the surveying phase took place. The interviewers received training sessions prior to the fieldwork to ensure that the communication of the questions to the respondent was clear and accurate.

A random sample of 1500 cultural tourists pursuing different cultural activities was obtained. The percentage of tourists approached that did not wish to participate was 10%. The sample was taken randomly from the general population of tourists visiting cultural sites in Havana. Interviewers followed a random number generator for approaching the contacted tourists in the last waiting room (sterile area) of the "Jose Marti" International Airport of Havana. This airport is the largest and most important airport in Cuba and receives most of the tourists arriving to the country. It was decided to conduct the survey at the end of the tourists' trip, as it increased the chance of obtaining the total evaluation of the travel experience. The airport was chosen because of the large influx of tourists, meaning that there was a likelihood of collecting the desired questionnaires in a short time. The surveys were implemented during four continuous months between May and October 2017.

All tourists that agreed to participate were informed of the following aspects in order to screen the target individual. The respondents were asked for the purpose of the visit in order to identify those focusing mainly on visiting Havana for cultural purposes. If the interviewees had not planned to visit historical or cultural sites, museums and/or heritage sites in this city, the interview was terminated. Finally, tourists were briefly explained the structure of the survey, the purpose of the study and the way in which they had to rate their perceptions regarding the destination. Table 2 shows the characteristics of the fieldwork and the structure of the questionnaire utilised.

Table 2: Fieldwork description

| Aspects | Description |
|---|---|
| Target population | International tourists visiting Havana for cultural purposes |
| Implementation | Face to face surveys |
| Structure of the questionnaire | A) Socio-demographic profile of respondents <br> B) Travel description and disposition to revisit the destination <br> C) Evaluation of Havana as a cultural destination |
| Place | International Airport José Martí, Havana, Cuba |
| Size and structure of the sample | n = 1500: Canada (28%); USA (10%); UK (10%); Italy (9%); Spain (8%); Germany (8%); France (8%); Other (19%) |
| Date of the field work | May to October 2017 |

*Source: Own Elaboration*

Tourists´ opinion of Havana as a cultural destination was rated through a seven-point Likert scale (1= I totally disagree; 7= Totally agree). Thus, tourists evaluated the city in terms of i) hospitality services, ii) tourist facilities, iii) service quality, iv) shopping, v) car rental/ taxi, vi) signposting, vii) conservation, viii) airport, ix) hygiene, x) noise, xi) massification), xii) promotion at local scale, xiii) conservation, and xiv) cultural activities.

## Data Analysis

Table 3 presents a description of the various methods utilised in the empirical analysis of the data. After coding the answers to the questionnaires, a t-test was employed to assess the differences between respondents in early May and late October. The former represented more than 70% of the total sample. The results showed no significant differences at the 0.05 level (Armstrong & Overton, 1977).

Frequency analysis was utilised to characterise the general profile of the respondent, their trip and future intentions. In order to reduce the number of variables, a confirmatory factorial analysis (CFA) was utilised on the fourteen variables that measured dissatisfaction. In order to infer about the research hypotheses formulated previously, a structural equation modelling (SEM) was employed. This is an appropriate technique for identifying linear regression relationships between several variables at the same time, to be expressed through hierarchical or non-hierarchical structural equations (Bullock et al., 1994).

Table 3: Methods utilised for data processing

| Method | Context |
|---|---|
| T-test | Earlier and late respondents |
| Frequency analysis | Socio-economic characteristics |
| Confirmatory Factor Analysis (CFA) | Grouping dissatisfaction-based features of the destination |
| Structural equation modelling (AMOS) | Hypotheses testing H1 to H9 |

*Source: Own Elaboration*

The theoretical model proposed in Figure 2 was validated in AMOS, a covariance-based SEM marketed by SPSS. Following Anderson & Gerbing (1988) and Fornell & Yi (1992), a two-step process was adopted. First, the factor structure of each of the four constructs of interest (DIS1 to DIS4) was assessed to determine the measurement model fit. Then, the observed factors (REVI and VISIT) were included in one full measurement model. Finally, the complete structural model was examined to determine whether the data fitted the theoretical model and test the proposed hypotheses. The $R^2$ parameter was utilised to evaluate the explanatory power of the variance of the two dependent variables (REVI and VISIT). Also considered were the values of the RMSEA (Root Mean Square Error of Approximation) index -which indicates the degree of adjustment of the theoretical model with the population covariance-, the degrees of freedom (df), and the CFI.

**Socio-Demographic Profile and Travel Planning**

Table 4 shows the results of the descriptive analyses of the variables "gender", "age", "occupation" "nationality" and "annual income". Only the most frequent categories are shown. The sample consists mainly of professional females. The most frequent age is between 25 and 30 years old, and more than 40% of tourists perceived annual incomes between 40,000 and 60,000 US dollars annually at the time of being interviewed. The average age of the cultural tourists of the sample is lower than found by Kline et al. (2016), but this is probably due to the fact that the reality of tourism in Cuba has changed drastically in recent years. Nevertheless, there are great similarities between the main outbound markets of tourism in Cuba (ONE, 2017) and the most frequent nationalities within the sample.

Table 4: Sociodemographic profile.

| Variables | Categories | Percentage |
|---|---|---|
| Gender | Male | 45.7 |
| | Female | 54.3 |
| Age | > 60 | 19.1 |
| | 45-59 | 12.8 |
| | 35-44 | 14.9 |
| | 25-34 | 39.4 |
| Occupation | Business owner | 12.8 |
| | Student | 21.3 |
| | Retired | 18.1 |
| | Professional | 30.9 |
| Nationality | Canadian | 28.0 |
| | US | 10.0 |
| | English | 10.0 |
| | Italy | 9.0 |
| Annual income | $50 001-$60 000 | 16.4 |
| | $40 001-$50 000 | 24.9 |
| | $20 001-$30 000 | 13.8 |

*Source: Own Elaboration*

Table 5 presents the travel description variables. We can observe a high number of tourists (47.4%) for whom this was the first time in Havana. Also, there were a considerable number of interviewees (36.8%) who had visited on at least four other occasions. The variable "length of the stay", measured as the number of nights spent sleeping at the destination, shows a great number of tourists (68%) with at least four nights, while the average length of stay in the country is 2-3 nights, according to official statistics (ONE, 2016). On the other hand, the visit to historical and heritage sites, and the search for knowledge on cultural traditions, are the main motivations of the cultural tourists interviewed. Almost half of the total sample was not willing to repeat the cultural visit to Havana. Finally, with regard the level of knowledge of the destination´s cultural promotion, a high percentage of respondents do not remember or have not seen or heard any cultural promotions of Havana in their country of origin.

Table 5: Travel planning.

| Variables | Categories | Percentage |
|---|---|---|
| Number of visits (VISIT) | ≥ 4 visits | 36.8 |
| | 1 visit | 10.5 |
| | First visit | 47.4 |
| Length of stay | more than 7 nights | 36.8 |
| | 4 - 6 nights | 31.6 |
| | 2 - 3 nights | 21.1 |
| | Less than 1 night | 10.5 |
| Motivation | Historic centre/Heritage | 78.0 |
| | Population/traditions | 71.0 |
| | Music/dance | 57.0 |
| | History | 55.0 |
| | Architecture | 53.0 |
| | Afro-traditions | 15.8 |
| Willingness to revisit (REVI) | Yes | 51.0 |
| | No | 49.0 |

*Source: Own Elaboration*

## Beyond Constraints: Tourists' Evaluation of Havana as a Cultural Destination

Tourists were asked about which aspects of Havana, in their opinion, should be improved in order to guarantee a satisfactory cultural experience. This was an open format question where tourists expressed their opinions. Table 6 shows the most frequent aspects highlighted by tourists. Tourist information offices, signposting and accessibility, and conservation and cleanliness were the most frequent problems. These aspects should receive greater attention from a tourism management perspective, in order to raise the image of the destination and improve the experience of the cultural visitor.

Table 6: Aspects that must be improved in Havana, according to cultural tourists 'opinions

| Items | Percentage |
|---|---|
| Conservation and cleaning | 45.0 |
| State of the roads | 44.0 |
| Information at the destination | 48.0 |
| Quality of the service | 41.0 |
| Food and beverage | 42.0 |
| Signage and accessibility | 47.0 |
| Accommodation facilities | 33.0 |
| Interpretation of touristic attractions | 33.0 |
| Shops and commerce | 83.0 |

*Source: Own Elaboration*

A confirmatory factorial analysis (CFA) was carried out for the fourteen attributes of the destination that were rated by cultural tourists (table 1). The CFA analysis allows the formal definition of the constructs of the model, distinguishing four areas of products and services that can be improved at cultural destinations. The first dimension (DIS1) refers to four negative aspects affecting tourist facilities and infrastructure at the cultural destination, mainly related to service quality; DIS2 is a construct grouping transport and roads´ weaknesses; DIS3 focuses on aspects related to the natural environment, massification and noise; and DIS4 dimension focuses on the need of qualification of the cultural products and services on offer at the destination (table7). In average, DIS 4 was the factor that received the highest score, which denotes that on-site cultural promotion, products and activities present important weaknesses at the destination, from the point of view of the cultural tourists. The rest of factors were also rated around 4.00, which means that tourists in general perceived problems with tourist facilities, transport infrastructure and hygiene.

All the factor coefficients were above 0.51, which indicates a high correlation inside the constructs. The overall fit was adequate (Chi$^2$= 136.12; df = 40) whereas RMSEA=0.079, CMIN/DF=1.00 and CFI = 0.978 were in acceptable ranges to confirm a correct adjustment to the data. To assess the measurement quality, the study examined both validity and reliability of the latent variables through the AVE- Average Variance Extracted.

Table 7: Results of the Confirmatory Factorial Analysis (CFA)

| Factors / Variables | Factor Coef | AVE | A.C. |
|---|---|---|---|
| DIS1 Problems with tourist facilities and infrastructure | 3.95 | 40.77 | 0.90 |
| Lack of professionalism in hospitality services | 0.81 | | |
| Facilities and infrastructures in bad conditions | 0.80 | | |
| Poor service quality in hotel, restaurants, etc. | 0.70 | | |
| Few shopping options | 0.67 | | |
| DIS2 Poor quality of transport, signalization and roads | 4.08 | 10.60 | 0.89 |
| Car rental/ Taxi unavailable | 0.87 | | |
| Bad signposting of roads and/or places of interest | 0.82 | | |
| Roads in bad conditions | 0.74 | | |
| Problems at the airport | 0.68 | | |
| DIS3 Hygiene and peace | 4.20 | 5.51 | 0.87 |
| Natural environment lacking cleanliness and conservation | 0.85 | | |
| Noise | 0.81 | | |
| Crowded destination | 0.77 | | |
| DIS4 Cultural products and services | 4.47 | 2.78 | 0.79 |
| Bad promotion of cultural events and programmes locally | 0.72 | | |
| Cultural attractions lacking maintenance and conservation | 0.63 | | |
| Cultural activities less developed or lacking a business approach | 0.53 | | |
| *Cronbach's Alpha total =0 .945* | | | |
| *Kaiser-Meyer-Olkin (KMO) = 0.914* | | | |

*Source: Own Elaboration*

By validating the path diagram proposed in Figure 1, the model indicated an adequate adjustment to the data without proposals for modifications. The measures of RMSEA=0.060, CMIN/DF=2.685 and CFI=0.987 were found to be acceptable to validate the model and its suitability to the data. Figure 2 summarises the general results of the model, the regression weights that were significant and the general indices of the model, as well as the test results of the hypotheses. The figure also presents the values of $R^2$ for the endogenous variables, which denote a high reliability of the measure, explaining 56% of the variance of VISIT, and 67% of REVI.

Figure 3: Results for the structural model.

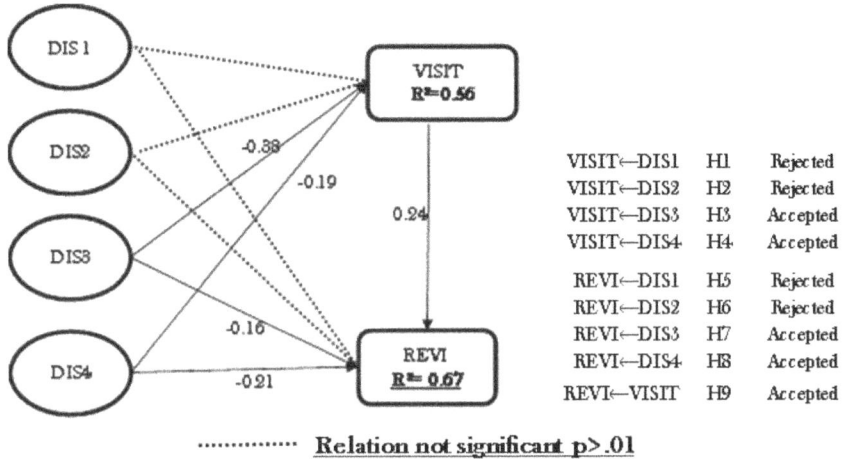

| VISIT←DIS1 | H1 | Rejected |
| VISIT←DIS2 | H2 | Rejected |
| VISIT←DIS3 | H3 | Accepted |
| VISIT←DIS4 | H4 | Accepted |
| REVI←DIS1 | H5 | Rejected |
| REVI←DIS2 | H6 | Rejected |
| REVI←DIS3 | H7 | Accepted |
| REVI←DIS4 | H8 | Accepted |
| REVI←VISIT | H9 | Accepted |

············· **Relation not significant p>.01**

*Source: Own Elaboration*

Only two dimensions resulted in having a direct and negative influence on loyalty variables (DIS3 and DIS 4). This denotes that the lack of conservation of the natural environment, the massification (DIS3) and the low quality of cultural products and services on offer at the destination (DIS4) are constraining factors for tourism loyalty, leading to the acceptance of H3, H4, H7 and H8. Other features related to tourism and urban infrastructure are found not to be relevant in explaining the loyalty of cultural tourists, leading to the rejection of H1, H2, H5 and H6. In addition, it was confirmed that repeating tourists are the ones who are more willing to repurchase the destination in the near future (H9).

In most destinations, tourism management usually focuses on those aspects that ensure satisfactory tourism experiences. This contrasts with evidence showing that tourists are concerned about socio-economic and structural problems of the destinations visited (Martín et al., 2014). This research has shown that a tourist's negative opinion of the conditions and level of conservation of the natural environment affect their actual decisions and future intention to repeat the visit, thus concluding that there exists a significant environmental awareness among cultural travellers visiting Cuba, and a resistance against the massification of this cultural destination.

Moreover, it has been proven that the set of cultural activities and services on offer at the destination is crucial to increasing cultural tourism demand, as it is a determining factor of loyalty. Consequently, cultural destinations must not only design a supply of products and services to be coherent with their values, but they also need to provide an outstanding cultural experience, by adapting tourist information and cultural programmes to the expectations of tourists, before and during the stay at the destination. At this point, planning not only exploits the advantages of having genuine heritage and history, but also attempts to minimise or correct possible unnecessary excesses in terms of cultural supply (i.e., mass cultural activities).

Based on the results of the structural model, loyalty was found not to be dependent directly on the quality of the tourism facilities, transport and roads; although past research has observed that these aspects are important components of the cultural experience (Cetin & Bilgihan, 2016). It opens up a new perspective for tourism managers, showing that there exist specific areas of the destination that enhance the cultural experience, although do not impact on a tourist's decision to repeat the visit.

## Discussion and Concluding Remarks

There is an indissoluble link between cultural heritage and tourism, and cultural tourism is neither against the protection of a place's heritage nor against the satisfaction of the local communities' needs. The success of this link depends on the responsible and sustainable management of the cultural heritage and on the capacity to generate a balance between the conservation of the heritage and the obtaining of social and economic benefits. In Cuba, there is huge potential for the development of cultural tourism, with tourists in this market segment have a high socio-economic level, who stay longer at the destination and spend more, on average, when compared to other categories of tourists.

From the theoretical perspective, the main contributions of this work are that i) it provides a better and wider understanding of the behaviour of cultural tourists; and ii) it identifies destination features that are relevant to explaining the loyalty of cultural tourists, highlighting the challenges that this represents for a cultural urban destination. That is, this research has shown that cultural tourists perceiving more environmental problems and noise contamination have visited the destination less and are less willing to repeat the cultural experience. In addition, there is an explanatory power of the influence of tourists' dissatisfaction with cultural services and activities on both the repetition of the visit and the willingness to choose the same destination in the near future. This evidence is novel and may allow policy makers to embrace useful recommendations for destination management, which can improve the profitability of marketing strategies.

Since tourist perceptions of the destination's weaknesses regarding the quality of the tourism infrastructure, the transport and roads do not have a direct impact on the repetition of the visit and the future intentions of cultural tourists, it does not need to become a priority within the strategies aiming to promote loyalty for the cultural segment. Nevertheless, these are key areas intervening in the conformation of the cultural experience, and thus affect the destination image, reputation and economic impact.

From a managerial and policy perspective, the loyalty of the cultural tourist could be increased by enhancing the quality of the cultural offer, improving cleaning and hygiene and the protection of the environment at the cultural destination. This question arises for certain key tourism destinations for which it is crucial to select key cultural activities according to the characteristics of the demand and develop appropriate information channels to guide cultural tourists on the appropriate time and area to enjoy a healthy and peaceful experience in the best possible conditions and with the highest consideration towards the environment. This requires close collaboration between tourism authorities, the tourism industry and other public and private actors, posing a challenge for tourism governance. Therefore, taking advantage of cultural values at the destination together with proper environmental management are the most important elements that need to be incorporated in the specialisation strategies of Havana.

This is of crucial importance at the time of this health crisis (COVID19) we are living; it is the moment for cultural destinations to decide how they want to re-adapt their tourism systems. The challenge is now to collectively learn from this global tragedy to accelerate the transformation of sustainable tourism. Some destinations will undoubtedly reconsider the nature of their tourism industry and focus more on local and sustainable forms of tourism, without substantial institutional and governmental interventions (Ryu et al., 2020). For the case of Cuba, government priorities, which are currently focussed on saving lives and creating conditions to restart domestic economies and education systems can be a limiting factor for efficient tourism recovery and resilience, while the juggernaut of international tourism will roll on.

This study has various limitations that substantially reduce the potential generalisation of its results and the scope of its conclusions. First, it is based on a single destination of cultural tourism, and therefore there is need to consider evidence on other alternative destinations in the Caribbean region. Moreover, the investigation of the areas of dissatisfaction, and how they influence past visits and future intentions, do require a more profound and detailed examination of their relationship with the cultural experience, satisfaction, image and expenditure decisions of the cultural tourists. Thus, future studies should investigate these effects, together with a more segmented approach of the demand in different types of cultural destinations. It is of crucial importance to consider that there exist traditional and emerging, coastal and urban cultural sites and that cultural tourists behave different according to their features. This assessment might be useful for suggesting segmented recommendations that would meet the specific requirements of the various types of cultural tourists and destinations.

Finally, the commercialisation strategies of Havana as a cultural destination will be more successful, insofar as they: i) take advantage of the most authentic resources of Cuban culture that make the destination unique, thus promoting creative cultural industries, ii) provide peaceful cultural experiences with a minimum impact on the environment and in the best possible conditions, iii) improve the capacity of designing high quality and more benevolent cultural products and services according to different cultural segments (i.e. micro destinations), iv) avoid massification and degradation of the urban infrastructure, v) implement efficient information channels online and on-site.

**Key Takeaways:**

- Bad signposting, conservation and cleanliness were the most frequent problems identified by tourists visiting Havana as a cultural destination.

- Tourists show higher levels of dissatisfaction with the on-site cultural promotion, shopping and signposting than for the rest of the attributes of the destination.

- Massification, and lack of hygiene, cleanliness and conservation of the natural/cultural environment have a negative impact on the number of visits and tourists´ intentions to repeat the visit, thus are constraining factors of cultural tourism loyalty

- The quality of infrastructures, transport, roads, and signposting do not have a direct effect on cultural tourists´ loyalty, although they are important components of a satisfactory cultural experience.

# REFERENCES

Akhoondnejad, A. (2016). Tourist loyalty to a local cultural event: The case of Turkmen handicrafts festival. *Tourism Management, 52*, 468-477.

Alegre, J., & Garau, J. (2010). Tourist satisfaction and dissatisfaction. *Annals of tourism research, 37*(1), 52-73.

Alarcón, C. C., & Hechavarría, L. T. (2016). Coherencia de la oferta turística de Cuba y la demanda turística estadounidense/Coherence of the Cuban tourist facilities and the American tourist demand. *Retos Turísticos, 15*(1).

Almeida-Santana, A., & Moreno-Gil, S. (2018). Understanding tourism loyalty: Horizontal vs. destination loyalty. *Tourism Management, 65*, 245-255.

Anderson, J. C., & Gerbing, D. W. (1988). Structural equation modeling in practice: A review and recommended two-step approach. *Psychological Bulletin, 103*(3), 411-423.

Armstrong, J. S., & Overton, T. S. (1977). Estimating nonresponse bias in mail surveys. *Journal of Marketing Research, 14*(3), 396-402.

Bonink, C. (1992). *Cultural Tourism Development and Government Policy* (Unpublished master's thesis). Rijksuniversiteit, Utretch.

Bullock, H. E., Harlow, L. L., & Mulaik, S. A. (1994). Causation Issues in Structural Equation Modeling Research. *Structured Equation Modeling, 1*(3), 253-267.

Caro, J. L., Luque, A. M., & Zayas Fernández, B. (2014). *Aplicaciones tecnológicas para la promoción de los recursos turísticos culturales.* Paper presented at XVI Congreso Nacional de Tecnologías de la Información Geográfica 25, 26 y 27 de Junio de 2014, Alicante.

Cetin, G., & Bilgihan, A. (2016). Components of cultural tourists' experiences in destinations. *Current Issues in Tourism, 19*(2), 137-154.

Chávez, E. S., Chávez, E. S., & i Cerdan, L. M. (2019). El Turismo en Cuba: Desarrollo, Retos y Perspectivas/Tourism in Cuba: Development, Challenges, Perspectives. *ROSA DOS VENTOS-Turismo e Hospitalidade, 11*(1).

Chias Suriol, J. (2003). *Del recurso a la oferta turístico cultural: catálogo de problemas.* Paper presented at Congreso Internacional del Turismo Cultural, Salamanca.

Cisneros-Martínez, J. D., & Fernández-Morales, A. (2015). Cultural tourism as tourist segment for reducing seasonality in a coastal area: the case study of Andalusia. *Current Issues in Tourism, 18*(8), 765-784.

Correia, A., Kozak, M., & Ferradeira, J. (2011). Impact of culture on tourist decision-making styles. *International Journal of Tourism Research, 13*(5), 433- 446.

Cruz Sosa, N. (2009). *Canadá, potencialidades para el turismo cultural en la Ciudad de La Habana* (Unpublished master's thesis). Centro de Estudios Turísticos, Universidad de La Habana, La Habana.

Csapo, J. (2012). The role and importance of cultural tourism in modern tourism industry. *Strategies for tourism industry-micro and macro perspectives*, 201-232.

Dávid, L., Remenyik, B., & Gergely, B. Z. (2013). Special interest cultural tourism products: The case of gyimes in Transylvania. In G. Richards & M. K. Smith (Eds.), *The Routledge handbook of cultural tourism* (pp. 283–291). Oxon: Routledge.

Figueras, M. A., & Pérez Cárdenas, Y. (2015). Competitividad del destino turístico Cuba: impacto económico. *Economía y Desarrollo, 153*, 178-189.

Fornell, C., & Yi, Y. (1992). Assumptions of the two-step approach to latent variable modeling. *Sociological Methods & Research, 20*(3), 291-320.

García, V. R., & López, L. V. (2012). Turismo en Cuba: desempeño reciente y evaluación de la participación extranjera. *Economía y Desarrollo, 147*(1), 185-202.

Gössling, S., Scott, D., & Hall, C. M. (2020). Pandemics, tourism and global change: a rapid assessment of COVID-19. *Journal of Sustainable Tourism*, 1-20.

Icomos (1999). *Carta Internacional de Turismo Cultural* (8 Borrador). Retrieved from the Icomos website: http://www.icomos.org/tourism/tourism_sp.html

Icomos (1976). *Carta Internacional de Turismo Cultural* (Report from Belgic, 1976) Retrieved from de Icomos website http://www.icomos.org/tourism/tourism_sp.html

Icomos (1964). *Carta internacional sobre la conservación y la restauración de monumentos y de conjuntos histórico-artísticos.* Paper presented at II Congreso Internacional de Arquitectos y Técnicos de Monumentos Históricos, Venecia.

Irish Tourist Board (1988). *Inventory of cultural tourism resources in the member states and assessment on methods used to promote them.* Brussels: DG VII. European Commission.

Jovicic, D. (2016). Cultural tourism in the context of relations between mass and alternative tourism. *Current Issues in Tourism, 19*(6), 605-612.

Kline, C., Bulla, B., Rubright, H., Green, E., & Harris, E. (2016). An exploratory study of expectation–importance–performance analysis with cultural tourists in Havana, Cuba. *Tourism and Hospitality Research, 16*(1), 19-34.

Lau, A. L., & McKercher, B. (2004). Exploration versus acquisition: A comparison offirst-time and repeat visitors.Journal of Travel Research, 42(3), 279e285.https://doi.org/10.1177/0047287503257502

López-Guzmán, T., Borges, O., Hernández-Merino, M., & Cerezo, J. M. (2013). Tourism in Cape Verde: an analysis from the perspective of demand. *Tourism Economics, 19*(3), 675-688.

MacDonald, G (2004). *Unpacking Cultural Tourism* (Unpublished master's thesis). Simon Fraser University, Burnaby.

Martín, B. G., López, X. A., & Ibarra, E. M. (2014). La información climático-meteorológica proporcionada al turista. Explorando el caso español. *Anales de Geografía de la Universidad Complutense, 34*(2), 97-117.

McIntosh, A. J., & Prentice, R. C. (1999). Affirming authenticity: Consuming cultural heritage. *Annals of tourism research, 26*(3), 589-612.

McKercher, B., Cros, H. D., & McKercher, R. B. (2002). *Cultural tourism: the partnership between tourism and cultural heritage management.* Haworth Hospitality Press.

McKercher, B., Wong, C., & Lau, G. (2006). How tourists consume a destination. *Journal of Business Research, 59*, 647–652.

Moreno, M. R., Molina, C. M., & Moreno, R. R. (2013). Satisfacción, lealtad y colectivismo en destinos culturales: Satisfaction, loyalty and collectivism in cultural destinations. *Tourism & Management Studies, 9*(2), 44-49.

Norval, A. J. (1936). *The tourist industry.* Londres: Ed. Sir Isaac Pitman & Sons, Ltd.

Oliver, R. L. (1999). Whence consumer loyalty? The Journal of Marketing, 63,33e44. https://doi.org/10.2307/1252099.

ONE (2017). *Anuario estadístico de La Habana.* Retrieved from the ONE website: http://www.one.cu

Pedersen, A. (2005). *Gestión del turismo en sitios del Patrimonio Mundial.* Francia: Organización de las Naciones Unidas para la Educación, la Ciencia y la Cultura–UNESCO.

Pérez Guilarte, Y. (2014). *Nuevas tendencias en turismo cultural. El papel de la investigación turística en ciudades patrimoniales: los casos de Santiago de Compostela y la Habana Vieja* (master's thesis). Universidad Santiago de Compostela, España.

Pérez Guilarte, Y., & Echarri Chávez, M. (2012). El Turismo Cultural, ¿Alternativa Turística para-Cuba? La Imagen de La Habana como Destino Cultural en el Mercado Español. *Journal of Social Sciences and Humanities, 2,* 33-50.

Pulido-Fernández, J. I., Cárdenas-García, P. J., & Durán-Román, J. L. (2016). Socio-economic profile of tourism expenditure in emerging urban-cultural destinations. *Tourism Planning & Development,* 1-19.

Pratt, C., & Tarlow, P. (2014). The Cultural Tourism Product, Meeting of Cultures: Safety, Security and Planning Guidelines. *International Journal of Safety and Security in Tourism and Hospitality, 1*(8), 28-35.

Ramseook-Munhurrun, P., Seebaluck, V. N., & Naidoo, P. (2015). Examining the structural relationships of destination image, perceived value, tourist satisfaction and loyalty: case of Mauritius. *Procedia-Social and Behavioral Sciences, 175,* 252-259.

Richards, G. (2018). Cultural tourism: A review of recent research and trends. *Journal of Hospitality and Tourism Management, 36,* 12-21.

Richards, G. (2011) Cultural tourism trends in Europe: a context for the development of Cultural Routes. In Khovanova-Rubicondo, K. (ed.) *Impact of European Cultural Routes on SMEs' innovation and competitiveness* (pp.21-39). Strasbourg: Council of Europe Publishing

Richards, G. (2007). *ATLAS Cultural Tourism Survey* (Summary Report). Retrieved from ATLAS website: http://www.dipalme.org/Servicios/Informacion/Informacion.nsf/1e588866373db7f0c1256ae200 2cd542/2777038571b6a4e6c125728100468ee4/$FILE/Summary%20ATLAS%20Cultural%20T ourism%20Survey.pdf

Richards, G. (2004). *Nuevos caminos para el turismo cultural.* Retrieved from the Tourism Market Trends website: http://www.diba.es/cerc/Arxinterac04/Arxsem1/richards/ponrichardsesp.pdf

Richards, G. (1996). Production and consumption of European cultural tourism. *Annals of tourism research*, 23(2), 261-283.

Rodríguez Domínguez, Mercedes (2002). "Contribución a la Historia del Desarrollo Turístico de La Habana en la Época Republicana hasta 1958". Tesis de Maestría, Escuela de Altos Estudios de Hotelería y Turismo, La Habana 2002.

Rundle-Thiele, S. (2005). Exploring loyal qualities: assessing survey-based loyalty measures. *Journal of Services Marketing, 19*(7), 492-500.

Ryu, S., Gao, H., Wong, J. Y., Shiu, E. Y. C., Xiao, J., Fong, M. W., & Cowling, B. J. (2020). Nonpharmaceutical measures for pandemic influenza in nonhealthcare settings international travel related measures. Emerging Infectious Diseases, 26(5), 961–966. https://doi.org/10.3201/eid2605.190993 [Crossref], [PubMed], [Google Scholar]

Shen, S. (2014). Intention to revisit traditional folk events: a case study of Qinhuai Lantern Festival, China. *International Journal of Tourism Research*, 16(5), 513-520.

Smith, M., & Richards, G. (Eds.). (2013). *The Routledge handbook of cultural tourism.* Routledge.

Timothy, D. J. (2011). *Cultural heritage and tourism: An introduction* (Vol. 4). Channel View Publications.

Toselli, C. (2003). *Turismo cultural, participación local y sustentabilidad.* Retrieved from the website Portal Iberoamericano de Gestión Cultural: http://www.gestioncultural.org/gc/private/analisisSectoriales/pdf/CToselli-TurCultural.pdf

Twining-Ward, L. (2010). *Cape Verde's transformation: tourism as a driver of growth* (Working paper). Washington, DC: World Bank.

Valle, P.; Silva, J.; Mendes, J. y Guerio, M. (2006). Tourist satisfaction and destination loyalty intentions. International Journal of Business Sciences and Applied Management, 1, 25-44.

Villalba Garrido, Evaristo (1993). *El Turismo en Cuba.* La Habana: Editorial Ciencias Sociales.

Zhang, H., Fu, X., Cai, L. A., & Lu, L. (2014). Destination image and tourist loyalty: A meta-analysis. Tourism Management, 40,213e223.https://doi.org/10.1016/j.tourman.2013.06.006.

Chapter 4

# Interculturalism at the Nexus of Culture and Tourism

*Renita Ferreira and Lisa Cain*


## Introduction

This chapter explores the definition of interculturalism and its distinction from multiculturalism. It highlights how interculturalism is the bridge between culture and diversity, and explains the intimate and vital relationship between interculturalism, culture, diversity, and tourism. As with any tourism experience concept, it is important to understand interculturalism from both the customer's side and the provider's side. Thus, explaining the importance of intercultural training and identifying best training practices for expatriates are discussed. These best practices are partially achieved through an examination and explanation of Bennett's Developmental Model of Intercultural Sensitivity. Finally, a look at cultural tourism through the lens of interculturalism and ethnorelativism is undertaken. The various typologies of tourists and their attitudes and approaches toward destinations are discussed. Finally, caveats are offered against ethnocentrism and examples are provided for the ramifications when tourists are ill-informed.

### Interculturalism

Interculturalism is a relatively new term that has been coined in response to the limited breadth and scope that multiculturalism has afforded in terms of diversity and inclusion among constituents in a given location. As ethno-cultural diversity becomes more pervasive in terms of both expatriates living and working in other countries, and individuals visiting other countries, it is important to understand the feelings of belongingness that are prompted by interculturalism. At its core, interculturalism endeavors to create a balance in diverse representation of individuals' rights and cultural relativism (Gagnon & Iacovino, 2016). That is to say that through active participation among all constituents in a given society, the goal is to achieve genuine consensus with regard to "the limits and possibilities of the expression of collective differences based on identity, weighed against the requirements of social cohesion and individual rights" (Gagnon & Iacovino, 2016, p. 117). The basic tenet of interculturalism is that all diverse groups come together to contribute to shaping the primary cultural feel and representation of a location, without the majority suppressing minority representations and opinions.

The construct of interculturalism includes cognitive, affective, and behavioral manifestations at several developmental levels, and second language proficiency or multiple language proficiencies are an added value. Also included are ethnicities, nationalities, cultures, and religions (Bedeković, Bosnić, & Jaković, 2014). Bedeković et al. (2014) argue "interculturalism necessitates an openness to the expression of culture of 'the other', including dialog as a basis for the understanding of another culture, resulting in comparison, interpretation, understanding and eventually acceptance" (p.474). Nussbaum (1997) cites Cornwell and Stoddard who write that they prefer the term interculturalism to the term multiculturalism and diversity since the latter is associated with relativism and identity politics. Interculturalism by contrast connotes the recognition of common human needs across cultures (p.82). Barrett (2013) defined interculturalism succinctly: "Interculturalism represents a broader program of change, in which majority and minority communities think of themselves as dynamic and outward looking, sharing a common objective of growing together and overcoming institutional and relational barriers in the process" (p. 80).

Interculturalism in its theory and practice serves as a means to deliver a more inclusive tourism experience that is beneficial to both host and tourist alike. The tourism industry has the potential to take a leading role in fostering intercultural understandings, where local uniqueness and cultural diversity are both seen as assets, contributing to memorable experiences and an excellent touristic product. To achieve this, the industry must confront the ways in which it can inadvertently produce meanings that exclude many from the narrative, by simplifying them into dominant, and commercial interpretations of culture and people. The questions that are begged are: 1) how do we construct authentic and unique meanings and places, as we reflect and design culture for tourism; and 2) how can the focus be on diverse experiences and direct human interactions, as opposed to the barriers created by tourism bubbles such as mass resorts or cruise ships?

**Interculturalism: Examining Culture and Diversity**

Culture is a notoriously difficult term to define. Apte (1994, p. 2000) summarized the problem as follows: "Despite a century of efforts to define culture adequately, there was in the early 1990s no agreement among anthropologists regarding its nature." Culture is a fuzzy set of basic assumptions and values, orientations to life, beliefs, policies, procedures and behavioral conventions that are shared by a group of people, and that influence (but do not determine) each member's behavior and his/her interpretations of the 'meaning' of other people's behavior (Spencer-Oatey, 2008). Smith (2007) asserts that culture has become a commodity to be packaged and sold like any other, and it is in this context culture has become synonymous with tourism.

Culture has two important components. The first is the visible or explicit component and presents itself in the form of behaviors, food, clothing, language, rituals etc. The other is invisible or implicit and is deeply rooted in values, beliefs, and traditions. For this chapter, culture will be discussed as an independent construct so as to explicate the relationship and the distinction of being cultural and appreciating culture from a personal and independent point of view, from being intercultural and appreciating and respecting a culture for its visible and implicit offerings.

Culture is closely aligned with geography and locale of the destination. There are as many cultures as there are nations and some in between. One can be a passive observer and appreciate culture from afar or be active and become interculturally involved in a culture. There are four approaches that every tourist focuses on when choosing a destination for pleasure or even work. The first is human-environment interaction. The second is spatial flow of people and products (tourists, accommodation, restaurants, transportation), and information and money, which unite areas. The third is landscapes resulting from natural processes such as mountains, rivers, glaciers and volcanoes. The fourth is physical which affects the savoir-faire of the tourist when visiting a destination for climate in the expectation of experiencing the warm and balmy breezes while sitting on a beach or viewing the snow-clad mountains while sipping hot buttered rum from a lodge on the mountain slopes.

When tourists travel whether it is for business, education, pleasure, medical reasons, religious beliefs, or sustainable development they are inextricably and unwittingly interfacing and interacting with cultures. One can have a multicultural perspective as a tourist and recognize and acknowledge the existence of other cultures or be intercultural and be an active participant in other cultures. Whereas in being multicultural the "otherness" tends to be dominant while as in interculturalism it is more of the recognition of "we" and opposed to "them". Hence the stance that interculturalism is at the nexus of culture and tourism. The analogy would be culture and tourism are the two faces of a coin, interculturalism is the metal on which those faces are embedded figuratively. However, interculturalism is not only significant for the tourist, it is true for the inhabitants in tourist destinations. Both perspectives will be reviewed.

The other suffix appended to culture is diversity. Reisinger (2009) argues the concept of cultural diversity which can be defined in numerous ways. Cultural diversity is most often referred to as:

- The variety of human groups, societies, or cultures in a specific region, or in the world as a whole.

- The mosaic of individuals and groups with varying backgrounds, characteristics, values, beliefs, customs, and traditions.

- Differences in race, ethnicity, nationality, religion, or language among various groups within a community, organization, or nation.

- The variety or multiformity of human social structures, belief systems, and strategies for adapting to situations in different parts of the world. (p32).

In summary, Reisinger (2009) strategizes two concepts: the social context of culture and the demographic concept of culture, of which the social concept has predominance over demographics. She alludes to the fact that various cultures are different because of their geographical location. For example, the aborigines in Australia and the Native Indian Americans are both indigenous cultures, but because of their geographical location are different in the essence of their culture. She also makes the argument that cultural diversity subscribes to multiculturalism and that different cultures should co-exist. However, interculturalists would argue that the world has moved on and multiculturalism is no longer adequate. The indigenous people of Australia and the USA coexist with the Eurocentric population, but they are not integrated. That recognition has prompted some scholars of multiculturalism to rethink their positioning of coexisting cultures as being adequate and are slowly shifting their world view to interculturalism. In short, today's interconnected world needs interculturalism.

**Interculturalism and Tourism**

Tourism is about places and spaces that are embedded in cultures, economies, and social lives of communities. In tourism, development, consumption, and experiential characteristics become interconnected within a given geographical location. The complex processes of tourism depend on the locale, be it a single community such as the Zulu tribes in Swaziland, Africa or a vibrant, bustling, and scintillating destination like South Beach in Miami, United States. The tourists that each of them attracts are diametrically opposed in perception, experience, and satisfaction, and hence, Gnoth (2007) made the case for branding of destinations to market their product to prospective tourists (Saraniemi & Kylänen, 2011). That would entail branding destinations according to the native or indigenous people, language culture, religion, social life, natural resources, landscapes, historical and heritage sites and not to be overlooked the economic impact on destination.

Tourism affords opportunities for individuals to visit culturally unique and diverse places about which they are curious, interested, or even enamored. However, this also presents challenges for local and global business operators in terms of satisfying tourists' expectations while staying true to the cultural norms of the location. During travel, tourists interact with and among individuals (both native and relocated) and the cultures that are inherent to the location. What transpires in an intercultural encounter may be beneficial to all parties, it or may have less than desirable results for one or both players in the tourism encounter.

With many organizations welcoming tourists, so much time and money are expended on warm ambiance, tantalizing restaurants, exquisite interior décor, lush landscaping, ostentatious amenities, and savvy technology, while often neglecting the vital fact that virtually every human interaction in the tourism industry is first an interpersonal and, quite often, an intercultural encounter. This intercultural interaction which is often referred to as a soft skill in the literature (Sisson, 2003) is side-stepped in lieu of other competencies, yet it is one that must be prioritized because a simple misunderstanding at any level in tourism can be destructive to the image of the that organization, brand, and destination. Intercultural communication skills, which are often subsumed under the nomenclature of attitudes, and overlooked, are the vanguard for the hospitality industry and especially for the tourism industry where the interactions are nearly always close and personal. Intercultural communication should be impeccable.

To combat these issues, intercultural competency should be developed at all levels of the tourism industry, so that when tourists return with memorabilia, they do so not only with the ones of physical importance and pride, but those of the mind as well, when exhibiting ostentatiously their behavior towards other cultures learned on their travels. How is interculturalism inculcated within the tourism industry is the million-dollar question? It is not trivial nor is it difficult if you subscribe to its tenets.

Attitudes are a prerequisite to transition favorably or unfavorably into interculturalism. The genesis of this stance is closely aligned with one defined by Fazio (1986), where he discusses attitudes, "as consisting of three interrelated components: an affective component involving feeling about a cognitive component involving beliefs and a behavioral intentions component" (p. 204). The affective component entails emotion, and feelings about a subject or an object. The cognitive component involves beliefs and values of a culture and is subjective in nature. The behavioral component is the objective factor and one that is observable as actions and executed as skills. The latter component is the most germane to the tourism industry, particularly with regard to its employees and their interactions with tourists.

## Interculturalism and Managing the Tourism Enterprise

Because of cultural differences, the management of companies operating in the global tourism and hospitality environment might have trouble relating to their employees' work style, expectations, and ethics. Known as expatriates, many companies send their employees abroad to work to help with regulation and implementation of corporate standards and culture, introduce new technology, and enhance skillsets. Problems may arise because of a lack of communication and differences in work style and ethics. Hospitality and tourism scholars have pointed to the need to better prepare expatriates for their time abroad (Causin, Ayoun, & Moreo, 2011). Someone's values and beliefs may preclude the understanding of others' behavior and attitudes. Many of the misunderstandings among people from culturally diverse groups may be due to ethnocentrism, which is assigning primacy to one's own culture and assessing others according to it. Ethnocentrism and limited knowledge about another's culture may prevent objective assessment and understanding of culturally different people. This lapse can pose serious consequences for the work environment.

In order to manage culturally different employees and attract culturally different customer markets, it is necessary to know the surrounding culture of that employee. Cultural differences among employees and customers can make or break the industry. If the industry is to flourish in the future, the managers of tourism's multinational companies need to be flexible and adapt to the growing number of people from culturally diverse groups. Tourism industry representatives need to be able to identify unique individual and cultural skills and utilize them appropriately. This is crucial because, according to Hepple, Kipps, and Thomson (1990), hospitality is interactive, involving the coming together of a provider and receiver. Therein lies the conflict because communication without intercultural competence could be destructive to the situation at hand.

Communication as a soft skill is often left "uncultivated". James and James (2004) defined hard skills as task-oriented competencies learned through education and/or training and soft skills as aspects of attitude and emotion that demonstrated through effective communication and interactions with customers and employees, and the latter have become increasing crucial even in the technical environment. Lee and Khan (2008) study global consumers' different service perceptions and preferences in the international hospitality industry. The findings indicate four major areas that become distinctly evident which include service preferences, customers' complaint types, customers' service recovery preferences, and word-of-mouth intent. These findings underscore the importance and significance of intercultural sensitivity to both residents' and tourists' cultures and therefore their needs. With multinational companies these findings should not come as a surprise, instead it should be an eye opener. Pullman, Verma, Goodale (2001), argue that "research has shown that customers from cultures and nationalities have different expectations from services and perceptions of the actual service delivered" (p.5). In a study by Chung-Herrera, Enz, and Lankau in 2003 while looking for competencies to groom future hospitality leaders developed a list of 99 competencies under communications were: "speaking with impact, facilitating open communication, active listening, and written communication"; and under interpersonal skills included "building networks, managing conflict, and embracing diversity" (p.23). The literature has indicated that soft skills are admittedly important; however more work needs to done especially at those entry-level positions in the tourism industry which includes hotels, restaurants, tour guides, tourist centers, and to a lesser degree those in the transportation business.

## Bennett's Developmental Model of Intercultural Sensitivity

To facilitate that change Bennett's Developmental Model of Intercultural Sensitivity (2017) is chosen as the framework for developing the strategy for educating and developing intercultural competency. The reason for the choice is most employers in leadership positions fail to understand that having intercultural competency cannot happen overnight. It is a slow process, as indicated earlier, that begins as early as childhood when formative judgments regarding inclusion and exclusion occur. What most training in interculturalism involves is a 'band aid' rather than a shift toward intercultural thinking, communication and action. That ill-serves both tourism providers and in tourists.

The DMIS stages (positions) are construed both in terms of basic perceptual structures vis-à-vis otherness and in terms of certain "issues" regarding cultural difference that tend to be related to each of the stages. The names of the stages refer to the issues, while the description of the experience of each stage refers to its perceptual structure. The first three stages of denial, defense, and minimization are ethnocentric; they refer to issues that are associated with experiencing one's own culture as more "central to reality." The last three stages of acceptance, adaptation, and integration are ethnorelative; they refer to issues associated with experiencing all cultures as alternative ways of organizing reality. Movement through the stages is not inevitable; it depends on the need to become more competent in communicating outside one's primary social context. When that need is established, it is addressed by building more complex perceptual structures that can resolve the increasingly complex issues of dealing with cultural difference.

Figure 1: Developmental Model of Intercultural Sensitivity

| Figure 1: Bennett's (2017) Developmental Model of Intercultural Sensitivity | | | | | |
|---|---|---|---|---|---|
| Ethnocentric | | | Ethnorelative | | |
| Denial | Defense | Minimization | Acceptance | Adaptation | Integration |
| One views their cultural experience as the only one that is real and valid. There is little to no thought of 'other.' | There is a 'we' are superior, and 'they' are inferior mentality. One feels threatened and is highly critical. What is strange or different may be labeled as stupid. | Other cultures are trivialized or romanticized. One tends to deny differences (e.g., 'color blind') and only seeks similarities. | One accepts but may not agree with other cultures. One is generally curious and respectful. | One 'sees' the world through the eyes of others and makes intentional changes to their own behavior and values. | One easily and fluidly moves in and out of different cultural worldviews. |

*Source: Bennett, M. J. (2017). Developmental model of intercultural sensitivity. The international encyclopedia of intercultural communication, 1-10.*

The DMIS offers global tourism and hospitality companies a guideline for assessing where potential candidates for overseas work are situated on the spectrum of cultural inclusivity. This may help to inform the organization whether or not the candidate is a truly viable representative of the organization. If an individual proves to be ethnocentric, more cultural sensitivity training will benefit that person, their organization, and the future tourists with whom they will interact. The threshold for overseas employment should be an ability to demonstrate curiosity and respect for other cultures, or other higher levels of ethnorelativism.

**Interculturalism and Cultural Tourism**

Cultural tourism can be defined as tourism that focuses on cultural attractions, activities and practices as major motivating factors for travel. It stems from the insatiable curiosity to experience up close and personal what is written history. Hunziker and Krapf as cited in the Encyclopedia of Tourism (2000) expressed this well when they pointed out, "there is no tourism without culture' (World Tourism Organization, 1995, p.6). It can include a number of sub-sectors, such as Heritage Tourism, Arts Tourism, and Indigenous Tourism (p.30). Cultural tourism has traditionally been difficult to define because of diverse and changing definitions of culture. The cultural theorist Raymond Williams (1983) points out "culture is one of the two or three most complicated words in the English language" (p. 87). This complexity is compounded by prefixing it with tourism.

Definitions abound with annotations of past and present traditions of the people, their history and heritage, peoples' ways of living, their creative expressions whether it is a display in works of art, expression or behavior. One of the more elegant and cultured of the humanistic definitions is expressed by Adams (1995), one "travels for personal enrichment" (p.32), or search for knowledge, however, the pleasurable element, experienced through the satisfying encountered at the destination, cannot be ruled out. Cultural tourism allows visitors to witness indigenous culture.

The cultural journey of a tourist starts with a mode of transportation that takes then from their residence to their destination of anticipation. The tourist's experience begins right at the doors of the train they board or the greeting at an airport, or at the port of a cruise ship. Experiencing culture does not begin at the arrival at a destination. It begins with the planning but more so with the first encounter of the mode of travel to the destination. All modes of transportation are subsumed under tourism, hospitality, and the service industry. Service comprises the customer, in this case the tourist, and the provider of service. With the advent of globalization, international travel has witnessed rapid growth Hence the encounters between tourists and providers have become more culturally significant. The service provider is trained for the job whether it is technology, communications skills or other service-oriented skills. Often neglected is the soft skill of being intercultural knowing how to navigate the different cultures that they are confronted with. Case in point the airlines, they greet in a generic format, often with a precision so stereotyped, it could be mistaken for dummy. On the other hand, the customer is looking for an experience based on preconceived expectation. If that expectation is not met, frequently it results in dissatisfaction and the loss of business. There is a stark difference in the service provided by airlines. Apparently, there is a better understanding and training of other cultures within some organizations.

The cruise industry has been considered one of the fastest growing segments of the global travel and leisure industry. They introduce people to new destinations. Riverboat cruises visit the smallest inner cities and towns where the local people have yet gone accustomed to visitors from land, they know nothing or may something. A well-designed package that combines a cruise and local tourism (e.g., culture and heritage) can stimulate customers' perceived tradeoff values. In addition, offering content related to well-being (e.g., walkways, organic/local foods, yoga, and meditation programs) could increase customers' interest and involvement in terms of wellness benefits (Ahn & Back, 2019).

With most international cruise lines, the crews on board hail from the four the four corners of the earth. Tourism and the hospitality industry have a high labor-intensive factor and a low productivity in comparison with other sectors, and technology can help to manage knowledge and information within this sector (Álvarez-Bermejo, Belmonte-Ureña, & Estrella-Ramón, 2016). These scholars highlight the benefits of using a new mobile application called RE2, that was designed to help service sector professionals with managing information related to customers and services, particularly with regard to their cultural backgrounds.

Fernandes-Morales and Cisneros-Martinez mention studies that focus on the three impacts they have on local community because of the seasonality. Of special interest for this argument would be the social impact (Gibson & Bentley, 2006). Recently, in an interview with the residents of Juno, Alaska, a very seasonal port, the residents were crying foul because of the negative social impact of cruises and tourism to the area. The tourists had no concern about their culture, their lives, their values, and their beliefs. Rather than appreciate the cultural heritage of the area, the tourists were simply there to have a good time. The residents scorned their behavior but were forced to stomach it due to the benefits of the tourism dollars. Neither side befitted form the interaction, and each only acquired bragging rights the tourist had visited a remote area in Alaska, the residents of Juno had made a profit meeting tourists who could not speak English and whose nationality was unknown.

Cruise companies are challenged to create differentiated cruise packages composed by a high-quality level of on-board services and shore-based activities (excursions) offering the chance of visiting new cultures and touristic attractions, together with integrated transfer to and from the ship (Brida, Riano, & Aguirre, 2011). But other than a glimpse into a new area, what these excursions afford in the way of interculturalism has room for growth. It seems that, often, the ports of interest are romanticized, but there is little effort put forth to engender ethnorelativism in terms of acceptance, adaptation, and integration. There tends to be a cultural homogenization, and American hegemony prevails all over the world. For example, even the remotest village in Nepal or South Africa is aware of Coke and Pepsi. This understanding of American cultural norms may offer Americans comfort when traveling abroad, but it does little to promote feel and representation of the destination, without the majority American culture suppressing minority representations and opinions that represent the place of interest. While the onus of burden ultimately lies in the interests of the tourists visiting the destinations, the individuals who book the cruise line excursions could provide educational material and offer culturally adaptive and inclusive suggestions, so as to engender feelings of good will among the people who visit the various ports and the people who live at the various ports.

A note of caution: While cultural tourism is exalting to the visitor, it can be detrimental especially to indigenous people who feel their privacy has been invaded, which can lead to stress amongst local people (Theobald, 2005), unless as Pike (1967) points out the emic approach is presented to the visitors which focuses on cultural distinctions meaningful only to its members. Theobold (2005) highlights that a stressful interaction occurs when contact is made with a different culture and poor communication exacerbates the situation.

Smith (1989) has constructed a typology for 'tourist impact'. She classifies tourists as explorers, elite travelers, off-beat or unusual tourists, the incipient mass, the mass, and the charter. With each category, stressful contact between the host and visitors were seen as proportionate to increasing numbers of disruption to the area. The most impactful were the charter tourists and the least invasive were the explorers. There is a great deal of alignment between Smith's typology for tourist's impact and Bennett's DMIS. The six types of tourist depicted in Smith's typology may fall neatly into the classifications of the DMIS, with charter, mass and incipient mass tourists representing the ethnocentric classifications, and the off-beat, elite and explorer tourists representing the ethnorelative classifications.

Of course, it is when ethnocentric tourists descend upon culturally different locations that problems arise. Perhaps the most glaring and important examples of where tourists should practice interculturalism and ethnorelativism to the best of their ability are the *frail* or the United Nations Educational, Scientific and Cultural Organization (UNESCO) Heritage Sites. These are destinations that are protected for the right of the indigenous people such as the Saami ancestral lands in Finland and are subsequently not frequented by tourists. Another example is the flora and fauna in the Great Barrier Reef in Australia –which needs environmental protection from too many visitors, lest the marine habitat succumb to over-tourism and a disruption of the delicate equilibrium that helps the reef to thrive.

Figure 2: Typology for Tourism Impact

| Figure 2: Smith's (1989) Typology for Tourism Impact | | | | |
|---|---|---|---|---|
| Tourist Classification | Amount | Ability to adapt to destination | Tourist Volume Increase | Tourist Impact Decrease |
| Explorer | Very limited | Accepts fully | | |
| Elite | Rarely seen | Accepts fully | | |
| Off-beat | Unknown, but visible | Adapts well | | |
| Incipient Mass | Steady flows | Seeks Western Amenities | | |
| Mass | Continuous influx | Expects Western Amenities | | |
| Charter | Massive arrivals | Demands Western Amenities | | |

*Source: Smith V. (Ed.) (1989) Host and guest: the anthropology of tourism. University of Philadelphia Press.*

Misinformation or assumptions about cultures is another hurdle for tourists and tourist providers. Ethnoentrism can lead to monetary fines, incarceration and even death. Case in point is the example of is the up to $700 fine one may incur if caught buying or chewing gum in Thailand. Another cautionary tale lies in the Andaman and Nicobar island in the Bay of Bengal. In 2006, two fishermen were fishing there illegally and were killed for the crime when their vessel drifted too close to the shoreline. While gum chewing and fishing may be permissible anywhere in a Western culture location, that is not the case globally. Awareness of and sensitivity to these norms is important for the prosperity of all players in the tourism equation.

The steps necessary to avoid these debacles are to focus on diverse experiences and direct human interactions and to ensure open and honest communication among the tourist, the expatriate employee, and the residents of the destination in question. Offering the appropriate information to inform the tourists of the cultural nuances expected in a location are pivotal for setting appropriate expectations of the trip. Educating service workers in the cultural diversity of the guests and the existing culture and identifying way to cohesively incorporate nuances of both will set-up the employee and the organization for success.

# Conclusion

Ultimately, what is vital to remember for tourism providers and tourists alike is that ethnorelativism and a move toward interculturalism above multiculturalism is the means by which all constituents in the tourism transaction will benefit. While it is unrealistic to expect every tourist to subscribe to the habits of an explorer or even an elite tourist, it is reasonable to expect curiosity of and respect for different cultures and their values, beliefs, and cultural nuances. And proper training for potential expatriates in necessary for the employee to thrive and the tourists to have a greater intercultural experience. Understanding that intercultural sensitivity occurs in stages and that progression through these stages is a process that occurs with time, information and exposure to people from other cultures is important for the success of tourism. Ultimately, it is vital to recognize that interculutralism is the primary cultural feel and representation of a location, without the suppression of minority representations and opinions by the majority. Representation of a culture in the form of hiring an individual is not enough. Tourism organizations must work toward the inclusion of the cultural feel of the destination through infusing the implicit values, beliefs and cultures of the location, in addition to including explicit physical representations of those cultures. Fostering interculturalism will ultimately lead to greater respect and understanding across all players in the tourism equation.

## Key Takeaways

1.  Interculturalism proposes that all diverse groups come together to contribute to shaping the primary cultural feel and representation of a location, without the majority suppressing minority representations and opinions.

2.  Both the visible and implicit cultural offerings are important for intercultural appreciation and respect. Coexistence is not enough.

3.  Communication is a vital soft-skill that, without intercultural competence, could be destructive to tourism interactions.

4.  Cultural sensitivity promotes ethnorelativism (acceptance, adaptation and integration) and discourages ethnocentrism (denial, defense and minimization).

5.  Properly informing tourists about a destination and its implicit values, customs and beliefs may help avoid legal ramifications and may help foster greater ability for tourists' adaptation to a destination, thus mitigating their impact on it.

# REFERENCES

Adams, G. D. (1995). Cultural tourism: The arrival of the intelligent traveler. *Museum News, 74*(6), 32-37.

Ahn, J. & Back, K-J. (2019). Cruise brand experience: Functional and wellness value creation in tourism business. *International Journal of Contemporary Hospitality Management, 31*(5), 2205-2223. https://doi.org/10.1108/IJCHM-06-2018-0527

Ali-Knight, J. M. (2011). *The role of niche tourism products in destination development.* https://www.napier.ac.uk/~/media/worktribe/output-209366/fullthesispdf.pdf

Álvarez-Bermejo, J. A., Belmonte-Ureña, L. J., & Estrella-Ramón, A. (2016). An innovative technology proposal for improving communication, social reputation, and service quality: A case applied to the hospitality sector. *El Profesional de la Informacion.25*(6):960-969.https://doi: 10.3145/epi.2016.nov.12

Apte, M. (1994) Language in sociocultural context. In R. E. Asher (Ed.), *The Encyclopedia of Language and Linguistics.* (pp. 2000-2010). Pergamon Press.

Barrett, M. (2013). Intercultural competence: A distinctive hallmark of interculturalism. *Interculturalism and multiculturalism: Similarities and differences*, 147-168.

Bedekovic, V., Bosnic, I., & Jakovi, B. (2014). An intercultural personnel competence in cultural tourism (Scientific Paper). Tourism and Hospitality Industry, *Congress Proceedings. Trends in Tourism and Hospitality Industry*

Bennett, M. J. (1986). A developmental approach to training for intercultural sensitivity. *International Journal of Intercultural Relations, 10* (2), 175-195. https://doi.org/10.1016/0147-1767(86)90005-2

Bennett, M. J. (2017). Developmental model of intercultural sensitivity. *The international encyclopedia of intercultural communication*, 1-10.

Brida, J.G., Riano, E., & Aguirre, S.Z., (2011). Residents' attitudes and perceptions towards cruise tourism development: A case study of Cartagena de Indias (Colombia*). Tourism and Hospitality Research, 11*(3), 181–196. https://doi.org/10.1177/1467358411415153

Cantle, T (2013). Interculturalism as a new narrative for the era of globalization and super-diversity. In M. Barrett (Ed.), *Interculturalism and multiculturalism: Similarities and differences. competence* (pp. 69-92). Council of Europe Publishing Encyclopedia of Tourism. Jafari, J. (Ed) (2000). New York: NY, Routledge.

Causin, G. F., Ayoun, B., & Moreo, P. (2011). Expatriation in the hotel industry. *International Journal of Contemporary Hospitality Management, 23*(7), 885-901).

Chung-Herrera, B. G., Enz, C. A., & Lankau, M. J. (2003). Grooming future hospitality leaders: A competencies model. *The Cornell Hotel and Restaurant Administration Quarterly, 44*(3), 17-25.

Fayed, H., & Fletcher, J. (2002). Globalization of economic activity: Issues for tourism. *Tourism Economics, 8*(2), 207–230.

Fazio, R. H. (1986). How do attitudes guide behavior? In R. M. Sorrentino & E. T. Higgins (Eds.). *Handbook of motivation and cognition: Foundations of social behavior* (pp204-243). The Guilford Press.

Fernández-Morales, A., & Cisneros-Martínez, J, D. (2019). Seasonal concentration decomposition of cruise tourism demand in Southern Europe. *Journal of Travel Research, 58*(8) 1389–1407. https://doi: 10.1177/0047287518802094

Gagnon, A. G., & Iacovino, R. (2016). Interculturalism and Multiculturalism: similarities and differences. *Multiculturalism and Interculturalism: Debating the dividing lines*, 104-132.

Gee, C. Makens, J. Y., & Choy, D. (1997). *The travel industry. The meaning, scope and measurement of travel and tourism.* International Thompson Publishing.

Gibson, P. & Bentley, M. (2006). Study of impacts: Cruise tourism and the South West of England. *Journal of Travel & Tourism Marketing. 20*(3/4), 63–77.

Gnoth, J. (2007). The structure of destination brands: Leveraging values. *Tourism Analysis, 12*(5-6): 345-368. https:// doi: 10.3727/108354207783227939

Hepple, J., Kipps, M., & Thomson, J. (1990). The concept of hospitality and an evaluation of its applicability to the experience of hospital patients. *International Journal of Hospitality Management, 9*(4), 305-318.

James, R. F., & James, M. L. (2004). Teaching career and technical skills in a" mini" business world. In Business Education Forum (Vol. 59, pp. 39-41). National Business Education Association.

Macleod, D. V. L. (2005). Alternative tourism: A comparative analysis of meaning and impact. In W. F. Theobald (Ed.), *Global Tourism* (pp 123-139). Elsevier

Nussbaum, M. C., 1997. *Cultivating Humanity: A classical defense of reform in liberal education.* Harvard Univ. Press.

Penco, L., & Profumo, G. (2019). Mergers, acquisitions and alliances in the cruise tourism industry. *Tourism and Hospitality Research. 19*(3), 269–283. https://doi.org/10.1177/1467358417742686

Pike, K. (1967). *Language in Relation to a Unified Theory of the Structure of Human Behavior.* 2nd edition. Mouton.

Pullman, M. E., Verma, R., & Goodale, J. C. (2001). Service design and operations strategy formulation in multicultural markets. *Journal of Operations Management, 19*(2), 239-254.

Reisinger, Y (2009). *International tourism: Cultures and behavior.* Elsevier.

Saraniemi, S., & Kylänen, M. (2011). Problematizing the Concept of Tourism Destination: An Analysis of Different Theoretical Approaches. *Journal of Travel Research, 50*(2), 133–143.

Sisson, L. G., & Adams, A. R. (2013). Essential hospitality management competencies: The importance of soft skills. *Journal of Hospitality& Tourism Education, 25,* 131-145.

Spencer-Oatey, H. (2008). *Culturally speaking: Culture, communication and politeness theory.* (2nd edition). Continuum.

Smith, M., Macleod, N., Robertson, M. H. (2010). Religious and spiritual tourism. *In key concepts in tourist studies.* (pp. 139-144). Sage Publications

Smith, M.K. (Ed) (2007). *Tourism, culture & regeneration.* Cromwell press.

Smith V. (Ed.) (1989) *Host and guest: the anthropology of tourism.* University of Philadelphia Press

Theobald, W. F. (2005). *Global tourism* (3rd edition). Elsevier Publications.

United Nations World Tourism Organization (2018). *International tourism trends* 2017. https://www.e-unwto.org/doi /10.18111/9789284419876.

Williams, R. (1983). *Keywords: A vocabulary of culture and society.* Fontana.

World Tourism Organization (1995). *Report of the Secretary General of the General Programme of the Work for the Period 1984-1985.* Madrid: World Tourism Organization.

# Chapter 5

# Ethics in Voluntourism: The Good, the Bad and the Ugly of an Industry in a Responsibility Crisis

*Friederike Hertwig and Carolin Lusby*

Volunteer tourism, often also referred to as "voluntourism", has emerged with the commodification of volunteer missions within the last two decades. According to Guiney and Mostafanezhad (2015), it is one of the biggest travel trends in the world. With this development, the focus shifted from the mission or give back project to the demands and needs of the tourists or volunteers themselves. This dangerous shift has allowed the attraction of millions of travelers all over the world every year.

The estimated value of this industry is USD $173 billion annually (Pariyar, 2017). It is a vastly growing industry that has hardly been regulated, which has led to concerns by key opinion leaders within the industry. Large tourism providers have discovered this industry as an opportunity for diversification of their product portfolio, and have tried to satisfy the demands of all tourists through: short-term missions, flexible starting dates, no preparation, no requirements for participation, and a large variety of projects to choose from. An all- inclusive vacation for anyone looking to "do good" or "make a difference". Over the last two decades, a profit-driven industry has expanded business models often at the expense of the weakest. Sustainability has not been the priority of commercial providers, which has led to a hidden network within the volunteer tourism industry.

By far the most popular projects have been ones involving children (Guiney, 2018). There are many projects focused on teaching children or working in orphanages. This work seems to be mainly attractive to young people that have good intentions and want to work abroad. Numerous problems have arisen due to operators not enforcing pre-departure requirements, which leads to untrained volunteers engaging with young children, or in some cases even infants. Unsuitable and inexperienced volunteers, child abuse and exploitation, corruption and child trafficking are some examples of negative consequences of this trend. This chapter will explore the world of volunteer tourism with an introduction to its development in recent years and an analysis of volunteer motivation. It will discuss the problems caused by an unregulated industry, and the issues emerging from this. Lastly, it will conclude with recommendations and resources for volunteers and anyone interested to learn more about this industry.

## 1.   The Evolution of Volunteer Tourism

In order to talk about the development of volunteer tourism, one needs to understand the development of the tourism sector, as well as the world of volunteering. In a way, both have always been linked. However looking at trend developments in both sectors the dependency becomes more apparent.

Throughout the 20th century, organizations such as churches and youth groups have been going on volunteer missions to give back to communities (Hertwig et al., 2015). Government programs established missions to promote world peace and friendship, such as the National Peace Corps Association, which was founded in March 1961. These missions are long- term projects that last for two years with the possibility of another year extension. This includes typically up to 2.5 months preparation for the volunteers. The selection process is based on the skills and expertise of each volunteer. Those programs focused on the cause and host communities they were benefitting. Besides the Peace Corps, many other governments established similar programs such as Voluntary Service Overseas (VSO), founded in 1958; Australian Volunteers Corporation volunteers (JOVC), founded 1965; and the Canadian Executive Service Organization (CESO), founded 1967 (Butcher & Smith, 2015). Critics say that these programs are a form of neocolonialism and not solely for the greater good of communities in need. On the other hand, Butcher and Smith (2015) write how the Peace Corps was established helping the newly decolonized states with their economic development. Therefore, it can be discussed from various angles, however the application process is thorough, and they usually have more applicants than placements.

Meanwhile, over the years, tourism became the world's largest industry according to McGehee & Wearing (2013). Mass tourism emerged as a form of travel where tourists did not have to mingle with host communities and were able to stay within their resorts with direct transportation means. These tourism structures and systems created tourism bubbles, which isolated tourists physically and culturally. The name "mass tourism," stems from the group sizes which kept increasing (Mgehee & Wearing, 2013).

However, these experiences over time did not feel unique enough, and some tourists soon sought a different way to travel. The emergence of mass tourism occurred in the second half of the 20th century. Soon after, in the 1980s, the counter movement of "eco-tourism" and other alternative forms of tourism developed (Callan & Thomas, 2005). Tourists were no longer only interested in traveling to faraway countries for a relaxing sun and fun vacation, but also wanted to get away from the masses of tourists for a more authentic experience. In addition, the question of sustainability and what impact a potential trip would have on host communities and the environment soon played a bigger role (McGehee & Wearing, 2013). Evidently, mass tourism was the total opposite of "eco-tourism," which was also known as a niche market within the tourism sector.

With airplanes being able to reach any corner of the planet within hours, the desire to go to places that have less tourists and boast more unique experiences was more and more in demand. During this time, non-profit organizations fostered volunteering further as they depended on donations and volunteers to fulfill their missions. The allure of having a unique experience attracted many people to these missions. By the end of the 1990s, more and more volunteers went abroad to help communities in need. Volunteers felt more comfortable to go with an organized group, such as a church group or an NGO, as these trips usually took place in unknown countries and cultures, which could scare volunteer travelers away. However, many of those missions were long-term missions, the availability was low, and timelines were not flexible enough for many young volunteers that still were attending university or school.

This problem was soon enough solved. According to Bennett, Collins, Heckscher & Papi-Thornton (2018), with the emergence of the internet, volunteers were able to find out about more placements within small organizations in remote countries that matched their interests. The internet made it possible for volunteers and providers to connect. Especially between 2000 and 2020, the volunteer tourism sector increased enormously. With this rising trend, it did not take long for commercial tour operators to take advantage of this demand.

As tourists sought more individualized experiences, tourism providers diversified their business models. The term "sustainability" moved into the forefront. According to Guttentag (2009), tourists' demand for charitable activities and "giving back" had increased over time, which led to large commercial tour operators trying to enter this market based on their prompt analysis. Compared to the mass tourism market with lots of competition and uncontrolled masses of tourists, volunteer tourism offered a niche, which can make one tour operator stand out from the other (Trihas, Antonaki & Kouremenou, 2014). This phenomenon of diversification is nothing new and happens in a lot of industries. In tourism it is especially important, and even more so in volunteer tourism. This is due to the risk factors involved in tourism such as political unrest and natural disasters, which can make a destination unsuitable for tourists from one second to the next. As volunteer tourism usually happens in less developed countries with higher political uncertainty, it is important to offer trips to as many countries as possible. Instead of relying on one product and or destination, the provider can rely on several different products in many different destinations. If one destination is not suitable to sell to tourists, or one product is not in high demand anymore, the company still has other options to fall back on.

## Two Voluntourism Approaches

There are in essence two ways to approach volunteer tourism: as an add on to an essentially mass tourism or other form of trip; or as a stand-alone volunteer trip.

With competition being so elevated in mass tourism, one example of diversification within the tourism industry is the addition of a volunteer activity. This is a low-cost activity but adds great value to a trip for tourists, for example an all-inclusive trip, like a cruise (see also chapter one this volume). This activity can be a short visit to a local orphanage or a beach clean-up, which involves one day or a few hours of visiting or helping, donating some money, and then leaving. Providers use it as a unique selling point to distinguish their product from others.

However, over the last two decades, the main form for providers to diversify was to enter the market of volunteer tourism altogether. For example, STA Travel, a British travel company with £62.63 Million in revenues in 2018 (Craft, 2020), provided volunteer tourism as part of their portfolio of products. Commercial tour operators with established sub-companies that act as sending organizations, jumped on the high demand. They started sending volunteers with an all-inclusive package to all kinds of destinations and projects. The packages included flights, food, onsite organization, and the work itself. Those all-inclusive packages were priced high, with volunteers paying up to USD $2000 for one week of volunteer work (Westendorp & Hofstee, 2017). However, not only did tour operators diversify, but so did providers that had originally only offered language courses. They now provided volunteer experiences, sightseeing trips, and internships abroad (Hertwig et al., 2015).

The issue of how to locate so many projects for the new volunteer tourists to engage in became a crucial point. With high demand of placements, providers took different approaches. Some contacted local agents to find local organizations and projects they could place volunteers in, others established their own subsidiary NGO that would take care of the onsite operations (Drobner, 2016). Figure 1 illustrates just how many intermediaries are involved between the community and the volunteer, but also the sending organization. The volunteer can, for example, see an advertisement to volunteer while at school or through their employer, then facilitating a connection to a commercial tour operator (sending organization). The projects they offer are found through a local agent that connects to the receiving organization, which works on several different projects. Many large tourism providers are not well established locally in less developed countries and rely on local agents to scout enough placements and local partners. Local grass-roots organizations have the advantage that they are already integrated into the community and have projects established. This makes it easy for the commercial providers to outsource the placement of the volunteer. It is also a low-cost option, as the commercial provider is not involved with the onsite operations (Drobner, 2016). Commercial providers often hold local organizations in exclusive contracts, so that they cannot accept volunteers directly, or from other travel agents. This makes local organizations dependent on the providers and vulnerable if the provider for example decides to back out of the contract.

Figure 1: Better volunteering better care, International Volunteering

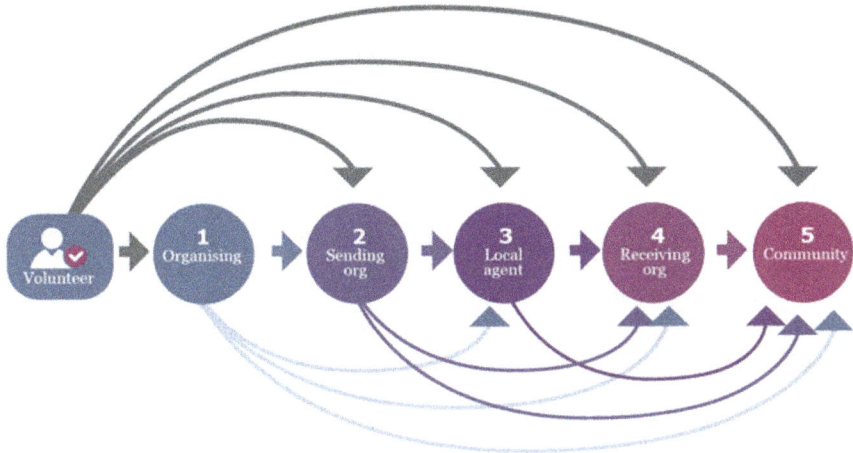

*Source: International Volunteering: Trends and Insights, 2014*

Nowadays volunteering is no longer only defined by traditional long-term mission, a local activity or missions provided by NGOs. Due to increases in demand over time, more and more commercial providers entered the market to be part of this lucrative business. It is now an easily accessible travel product, offered by hundreds of providers. What was once a niche market for commercial providers, NGOs and other organizations to diversify their businesses, has now been identified as one of the biggest travel trends in the last decade (Sin, Oakes & Mostafanezhad, 2015). International Volunteering HQ (IVHQ) for example, started off as a start-up company in volunteer tourism in 2007. In 2018 it was reported that the founder had sold 80% of the shares to an investment company. The exact value of the sale of his stake is unknown, but this investment company only invests in companies worth between $USD 50 – 200 million (Baker, 2018), which illustrates the boom within the industry.

Even though this trend came from the need in tourism to seek a more meaningful experience, its actual sustainability has been questioned in recent years. The focus instead has been on the volunteer and their experience, and not the sustainability of the project. For example: A turtle release project seems more attractive to young people when they can take a picture of how they are releasing a little turtle on a beach with white sand and turquoise water, rather than releasing them during the night with no light. However, volunteers that do their research know that turtles are only supposed to be released during the night, so they are less vulnerable to predators and the sun (Nahill, 2018). Incidents like these have caught the attention of the media in the past and lead to more questions about the sustainability of these volunteer activities. Information is not always made available to volunteers, as commercial providers are not fully transparent about where funds go, and where and what exactly the volunteers will be doing. The reasons for this will be discussed imminently. Hence, it is up to each volunteer to do thorough research and demand information when choosing a volunteer provider. Unfortunately, the motivation of each volunteer is different and thus not every volunteer is aware of unsustainable placements.

## 2. Motivations and Intentions

The motivations and intentions of volunteers are far more complex than they may seem. There are many reasons for people to decide to go abroad and volunteer. Research agrees that generally most volunteers do have good intentions. This is despite the negative side effects, which volunteers may not be aware of when deciding to volunteer. As mentioned, commercial providers make it difficult for the volunteers to access all information and there is a general lack of transparency. Providers lure volunteers to book through accessible and easy to book all-inclusive packages.

The "Better Volunteering Better Care" initiative, led by the Better Care Network and Save the Children UK, published a paper in 2014 that lists the different motivations by volunteers. The survey revealed that the main reasons to volunteer are:

- Personal Growth

- Giving back

- Bearing witness of poverty

- Learning and cultural exchange

- Desire to help directly

- Adventure

- Contributing to a social cause

When discussing key motivations, it is important to mention that 80% of volunteers are women, according to Mostafanezhad (2014). Also, it was found that women are more likely to volunteer to benefit others, whereas men are more likely to volunteer when it will benefit themselves (Gil-Lacruz, Marcuello & Saz-Gil, 2018). Over time, the urge of doing good while travelling seemed the perfect combination for young people to add to their resume. It almost reached a point where young people saw it as a requirement for future employers to show their commitment to the international community. The commercial providers made it easily accessible for everyone to go, as the starting dates were flexible, and the length could be as short as one week. The extra-curricular activity is hence contributing to their personal growth for their potential future job. However, Foller-Carroll and Sylvain Charlebois (2015) found that a volunteer would not solely volunteer to enhance their resume, altruistic intentions, and a general interest in "giving -back" also played a role.

Furthermore, through their experiences abroad, volunteers feel a form of personal transformation, as they experience different cultures, see a different perspective and build new relationships with strangers (Coghlan & Weiler, 2015, Foller-Carroll and Sylvain Charlebois, 2015). This transformation can also change their approach to certain situations upon their return home. Their thinking might be shifted in relation to consumption due to the poverty they experienced firsthand. They might feel different about common behaviors of their friends that now might seem wasteful. All these experiences also contribute to their personal growth. Also, in relation to this, recent findings of Francis and Yasué (2019) showed that most volunteers are driven to volunteer for personal growth. Their research indicated that volunteers sought "personal socio-emotional growth", which supports the findings of the Better Care Network.

With the introduction of social media, which allowed for easy access to information through the internet, volunteers have better insights about international development work done by volunteers abroad. Another factor of influence on young people is that female celebrities support international aid organizations or even go to a "Third World" country and report from situations onsite through social media (Mostafanezhad, 2014). Being able to upload images and videos live onsite is enabling young people to show off their experiences and contributions to social causes. When these friends read about their favorite celebrity also helping poor communities, it creates an incentive in young people to go out there and do the same.

For many volunteers, the hurdle of overcoming their fear of going into an unknown country far from their home is much higher. There are factors that might hinder them from choosing a destination, such as a culture that is unfamiliar to them (cultural distance), potentially putting themselves in danger, an uncertain political situation which may be different from home, or the heightened levels of poverty in a particular country. Through the commodification of volunteer tourism, providers take all these fears and constraints away from the volunteer. Even the time constraint that many volunteers have, since they are still in school or university, is solved through offering short term volunteer trips. Their motivations can be caused by good intentions but may also be due to envy of a friend who went there and got many positive comments and "likes" on social media based on their postings. The excitement to visit a country that tourists usually would not visit is high, especially since many previously untouched places have become so easily accessible. This would support the reason of adventure for volunteering as well as the desire to help directly and bear witness of poverty.

There can also be a combination of reasons, which as previously mentioned, makes the motivation of volunteers more complex. The importance of motivation has become very clear in recent years. Key opinion leaders within the industry agree that in order to make an experience more valuable for host communities and the volunteer, the volunteer should clearly identify his or her own motivations. The book "Learning Services the essential guide to volunteering abroad" by Bennett et al. (2018) talks about how to identify your motivation. It lists some questions you should ask yourself, and what motive might usually be considered "red flags". The authors highlight the motivations that might not match well with going abroad, and state that those motivations might also have negative consequences. The red flags they list are:

- Seeking a geographic solution to an emotional problem

- Looking to convert others to your faith

- Simply needing something that looks good on a resume

- Wanting to rescue poor people and "lift them out of poverty"

- Seeking to practice beyond your skillset

- Needing a vacation

The book's key message is to see the volunteer experience as a learning experience. It is an opportunity to learn about other cultures, communities, and about how to support others. Volunteering should teach about differences and similarities, about approaches, views, and values of other countries. Every volunteer has different motivations, but with thorough research and asking yourself the right questions, this experience can be helpful for volunteers and host communities. As previously mentioned, one of the main problem lies in the supply of placement opportunities and the way they are advertised and designed. Commercial providers design the projects for the volunteers' self-interest and not to have sustainable impacts on host communities (Francis & Yasué, 2019).

## Matching Processes of Volunteers and Projects

With no regulations in place, unskilled volunteers are matched with projects that would usually require a set of proficiencies. In many cases, the commercial tour operators do not know or check how sustainable the project really is. As displayed in Figure 1, the sending organization can be three steps away from the local community, not understanding their needs properly. The commercial provider relies on the local agent or the receiving NGO. Since their main interest is to place as many volunteers into projects as possible, and they do not thoroughly select their projects, they cannot match volunteers with the placements based on skills properly. Untrained, unexperienced, and often as young as 16 years old, volunteers get placed into the project of their own desire. Providers hide where the volunteers will go exactly, as they cooperate with local companies, that in some cases receive volunteers directly. In order not to harm their own business, volunteers usually only get to know where and in which project they will be involved in once they have arrive onsite. Apart from the poor selection process, this hinders a proper preparation for the volunteer. With no knowledge about the community or the projects, volunteers leave their home with good intentions to help, but virtually unprepared.

Conclusively, profit-driven providers design volunteer programs so that anyone who wants to volunteer can do so. Online marketing focuses on the experience and benefits for the volunteer and not on the host communities. Poverty marketing has often been associated with volunteer travel providers, showing images of children and communities in need. The entire marketing program concentrates on the fact that volunteers get the chance to help the poor (Wilkinson, McCool & Bois, 2014), which fuels the neo-classical stereotype and pushes volunteers into the role of saviors.

A study, done by Hertwig et al. (2015), investigated 23 volunteer tourism providers , which included a range of 44 corresponding volunteer products. Three years later in March of 2018 this research was repeated and 50 products of 25 travel providers were studied (compare Figure 2 and 3). Generally, there has been very little improvement over the last few years in the selection and matching of volunteers and projects. In 2018, 76% of the providers did not require a CV, 100% did not require an interview of any kind and 82% did not require a letter of motivation. This leads to concerns based on what was explained in the previous section: Identifying the motivation of volunteers is very important to have a higher chance of positive impacts on host communities and the volunteers. Furthermore, CV's, letters of motivation, references and interviews should be required to match volunteers based on their skills to the projects. This study also revealed that, to teach English, there were no requirements to send a certificate for proof of language skills or to obtain a language test provided by the tour operator. In 2015, 14% required advanced language skills. Compare this to 2018, where only 4% required that language level. This raises questions regarding the ability of the volunteer to properly teach a child English, when they might not speak fluently, or have any sort of education in teaching?

Figure 2: Selection process requirements by providers for volunteers in 2018

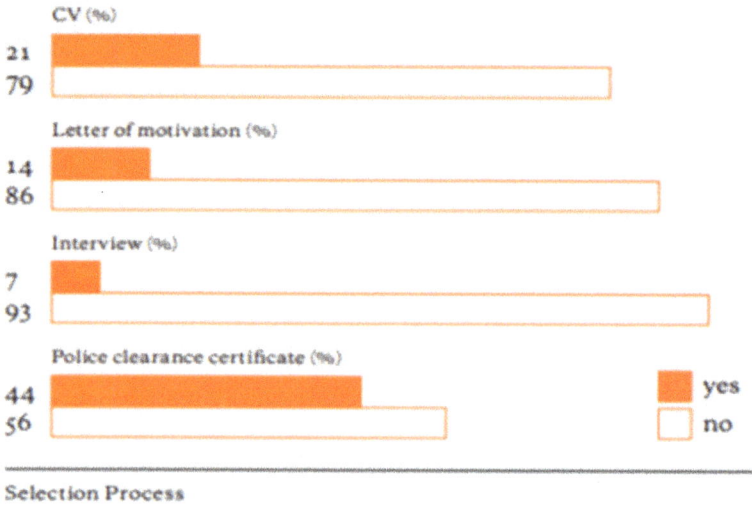

CV (%)

21
79

Letter of motivation (%)

14
86

Interview (%)

7
93

Police clearance certificate (%)

44
56

■ yes
□ no

Selection Process

*Source: From Volunteering to Voluntourism, 2015*

Figure 3

CV (%)

24
76

Letter of motivation (%)

18
82

Interview (%)

0
100

Police clearance certificate (%)

54
46

■ yes
□ no

Selection Process

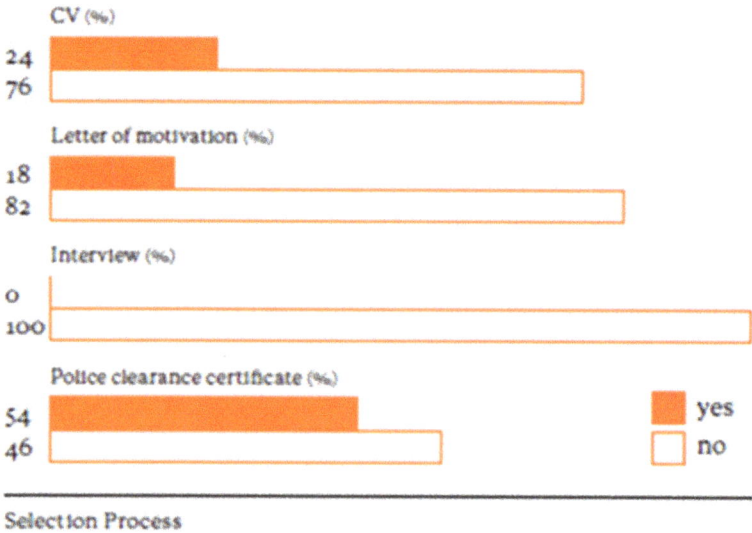

*Source: From Volunteering to Voluntourism, 2018*

It is hard to imagine parents in a Westernized country allowing unskilled and untrained 16-year-olds to teach their children in school. One can argue that there is a lack of teachers in communities and they might depend on volunteers. This might be a valid argument but does not lessen the need for volunteers to demonstrate qualifications such as advanced language skills and educational capabilities. With such skills and a good preparation before the beginning of the project and a thorough guidance onsite, this could lead to positive and sustainable impacts on the children. With no experience in teaching or speaking the language, children might repeatedly learn the same content every other week. In the worst-case, volunteers might even teach students false knowledge.

In both studies of 2015 and 2018, the vast majority of projects started every one to three weeks. This proves the flexibility that providers try to offer, which also means a high turnover of volunteers. Another issue is the preparation process that in many cases must be booked separately for an additional charge and is not mandatory, which can discourage volunteers from booking it. One of the largest providers, IVHQ heavily advertises an outsourced company for their preparation course. Further investigation shows that the preparation company is owned by the same founder of IVHQ, which shows that this is just an additional source of income for the owner (Drobner, 2018). Only for 16% of the providers does this preparation last one whole week (21% in 2015). Most preparations last for 1-2 days. The preparation includes courses on the culture and local language of the host community. It does not teach essential skills for the upcoming work such as teaching skills, which would be impossible to teach in one or two days. These findings are alarming and prove the statements of key opinion leaders that providers completely design their products to attract and accommodate as many volunteers as possible, and do not focus on the essential: the community it should be benefiting.

The range of projects is very large and can include environmental work, the medical field, animal rescue, work with children, such as teaching English, working in care centers and many more. However, childcare has been the most favored projects for young volunteers (Guiney, 2018). Due to the popularity of these projects, there have been a lot of arising issues that every volunteer should be aware of, as otherwise they might do more damage than good with their well-intended work.

## 3. Work with Children: An Ever-Popular Volunteer Experience

Many projects that providers offer involve children. Volunteers can work in day care centers, orphanages, teach in schools or get in touch with children by working in communities through other projects. However, the most harming form of volunteering is orphanage tourism. Guiney and Mostafanezhad (2015) identify orphanage tourism "as the donation of money and goods, attending performances, or volunteering on a short-term basis at orphanages as part of one's holiday". Many orphanages around the world are visited by tourists for a couple of hours as part of their travel itinerary. Often children are performing dancing and singing acts, dressed in traditional clothing. Tourists donate money and supplies to the orphanage. As previously demonstrated in Figure 1, in many cases intermediaries are selecting the projects for providers and hence they do not know or check how sustainable the project really is. The trend of volunteer tourism has been arising in such a fast pace, that large companies want to get involved quickly without thinking about the consequences or having done the necessary research. Therefore, they turned to local agents such as local NGOs to find suitable projects. Since they are profit-driven, their first interest is not the work itself and its impact. They care to create a product that attracts as many travelers as possible in a short period of time. To generate as much profit as possible, they supply the projects with the highest demand. That demand is fueled by poverty marketing, making motivated volunteers feel encouraged to go and help poor children displayed on websites and catalogues. With no selection processes or requirements in place, untrained volunteers find themselves working directly with, and caring for, often traumatized children in orphanages. This can be a very difficult situation for both volunteers and children. Volunteers are at risk of being overwhelmed by taking care of children with often special needs, as they have been separated from families and do not have an appointed primary caretaker. Most orphanages are understaffed, and workers are non-professionals. With overwhelmed local staff, volunteers have often witnessed child abuse with no one to report to. Since the initial sending organization relies on local partners, they do not feel responsible. Large volunteer providers blamed others involved further down the supply chain when faced with criticisms expressed by key opinion leaders.

According to the Better Care Network Netherlands (2017), 8 million children live in orphanages. A study done by UNICEF in 2011 concluded that 80% of orphans worldwide have at least one living parent. The podcast "Good intentions aren't enough: ending orphanage tourism" from November 2019 states that 60% of Americans still believe that orphanages exist in the United States, even though those were replaced with a foster care system about 50 years ago. They also mention that US passport holders are the number one contributor to orphanage tourism. The main contributors to orphanage tourism from the US are gap year travelers, students engaging in global service learning, funding from churches and support from short-term mission teams (Rethink Orphanages, 2018). However, the United States is the only country in the world that in 2017 implemented a whole-government strategic action plan for improving the lives of vulnerable children overseas (Rethink Orphanages, 2018). The Australian government considers volunteering in orphanages a form of slavery (Bekele-Piper, 2019), which shows the true extent of the problem is being recognized by many countries. Nevertheless, although all countries agree that orphanages are not an adequate child care system, most orphanages in developing countries (such as Cambodia or Nepal), are sponsored by Western donors and travel agents (The Love you Give, 2019 & Guiney, 2015). Volunteers do not know this, but they are "contributing towards a system of inequity, poverty and violence" (Bekele-Piper, 2019). But how exactly are they doing this?

## The Case of Cambodia

With the rise of volunteer tourism, there was globally an increasing demand for working in orphanages, however there were not enough orphanages. For example, in Cambodia, this demand was seen by local agents and more and more orphanages began to be opened over the years. Most of them were not registered with their governments. The perception of tourists about Cambodia is that the country is generally poor, which gives tourists the incentive to help. Hence, Cambodia is one of the most popular countries for orphanage tourism. According to Guiney (2015), the number of registered orphanages rose from 154 to 269 centers in Cambodia between 2005 and 2010. But speculations are that there are over 500 orphanages that are not registered with the government. The number of children in these centers almost doubled during that time (Guiney, 2015). But where do these children come from? Figure 4 below illustrates an extended version of Figure 1. Brokers, otherwise known as "child finders", go out to poor communities and offer parents money for their children, promise the parents to provide better education for their children and take them to a better environment (U.S Department of State Office to Monitor and Combat Trafficking in Persons, 2018). The parents are often poor or ill, which makes it hard to care for their children. The offer of the brokers seems like a good solution to the parents (Guiney, 2015). This confirms Coates' notion (2005, quoted in Guiney, 2015) that some children end up on the street due to economic hardship because they must provide for their families, which could potentially lead to being trafficked and sold. By transporting the children into orphanages, it becomes officially a crime of trafficking, as victims are moved from one location to another, which in itself is categorized as trafficking (Trafficking in persons report, 2019). This results in a large number of unrelated children living in the same building, with unprofessional care takers, and contributes to children not being able to form an emotional attachment with one primary caretaker (Comhlamh and the volunteering and orphanages working group, 2019). The issue of trafficking of children to orphanages due to tourism was also addressed in the 2019 Trafficking in persons report.

Orphanages harm the health and development of children, exposing them to a greater risk of violence, neglect, abuse, and trafficking. It is recognized as the most harmful form of volunteering (Westendorp & Hofstee, 2017). A different set of volunteers arrive at the orphanage every week to try and form an emotional connection with the children, that soon after is broken again. Children need one primary caretaker, which is not provided in the orphanage and they subsequently form severe attachment-disorders. Children surrounded by only volunteers may develop severe disorders in social-emotional development (Westendorp & Hofstee, 2017). This can lead to significant cognitive and developmental delays (Comhlamh and the volunteering and orphanages working group, 2019). Studies have further shown that institutionalized children suffer from underdevelopments of weight, height, and head measurements, hearing and vision problems or delayed motor skills (Comhlamh and the volunteering and orphanages working group, 2019). This shortens the life expectancies of children in institutionalized care. Furthermore, directors of orphanages keep children in poverty on purpose, to attract more donors. A malnourished child attracts more attention than a healthy looking one. They are taught to smile and engage with the tourists. Contact with their families is prohibited and children must pretend they do not know where they come from (The Love you Give 2019). Guiney (2015) confirms that children are engaging in emotional labor to attract tourists to gain more funds for the orphanage. Out of the $USD 2000 that the volunteer paid, not much reaches the children, but instead ends up going to all the intermediaries involved, as shown in Figure 4.

Figure 4: Adjusted illustration by Better volunteering better care,

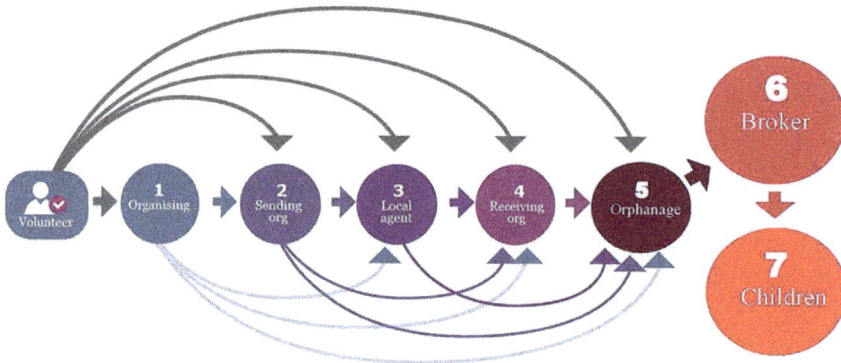

*Source: International Volunteering: Trends and Insights, 2014*

With no regulations for this industry in place, there is also no protection of children within volunteer tourism. Ruth Wacuka, a former orphan, talks about not being able to report child abuse to any of the staff members, which confirms the reports of volunteers (Bekele-Piper, 2019). The ethical question of allowing children one on one interaction with tourist volunteers unsupervised also arises. Sadly, many volunteers in orphanages or engaged in teaching are left alone with children. Onsite staff allows tourists to go on a walk or away from the premises with children (Guiney, 2015). Hertwig et. al (2015), found that only 44% of researched products required the volunteers to have a criminal background check performed, three years later there was a slight improvement with 54% requiring it (compare Figure 2 and 3). This is an improvement, however, considering that volunteers get exposed to vulnerable children, 100% of projects engaging with children should require this check.

Figure 5: Example of children used in advertisement promoting intimacy and physical contact between volunteers and children

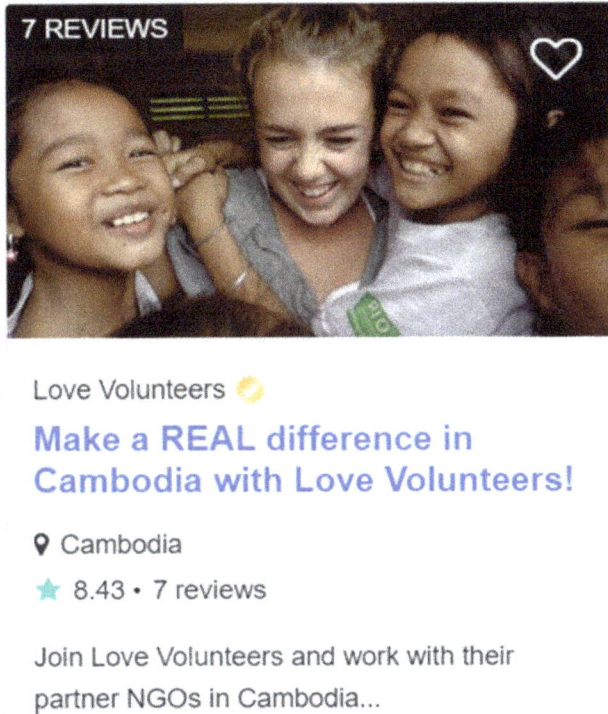

*Source: https://www.gooverseas.com/volunteer-abroad/cambodia/love-volunteers/22202, accessed April 20ᵗʰ, 2020*

An additional problem is the marketing and promotion of volunteering with children. Through marketing mechanisms, providers promote intimacy with children, where volunteers are displayed in close contact with sometimes even infants (compare Figure 5). In Figure 5, you can see a volunteer hugging several children tightly, which promotes physical contact with children. They are cuddling or holding hands. Displaying this image disregards the privacy of the child, hence is undermining the Rights of the Child. Marketing is using poverty to trigger volunteers' emotion and make them believe they can bring a smile to these children, too. These highly unregulated institutions offer no protection to the children involved, which puts them at high risk of sexual exploitation. In a police survey in eleven countries, ten of them reported cases of sexual abuse of children through volunteer tourism (Czarnecki , 2018). Children have become a tourist commodity, a commodity for people from developed countries to use to feel good about themselves.

Every country in the world has committed to family-based care, meaning orphanages in the long run should not exist (The Love you Give, 2019). UNICEF published Guidelines for the Alternative Care of Children (United Nation, 2010), which gives guidance for what should happen when children lose their parents. The first choice should always be to stay within the community, with a family relative or even a neighbor. The last resource should be an orphanage or a foster care family. Children should have a choice, and millions of children do not have that choice and get sent away to orphanages. Sending children away because of food or education should not be done and there are organizations in place to try and help as many parents in need as possible, in order to prevent them from sending their child away. As Ruth Wacuka states, volunteers do not have the ability to end poverty and help these children (Bekele-Piper, 2019). Material donations are a temporary fix but not a long-term solution. Orphans get kicked out of the orphanages when they reach the age of 18 and have nothing in their hands to build a future. No solid education, no financial support, many lost contacts to their families as it is mainly prohibited and hence, they have nowhere to go. The cognitive and physical damage they take away from being brought up in an orphanage adds to the disadvantages once they leave these institutions.

Volunteers are encouraging child trafficking by volunteering in orphanages, which is not sustainable and thus should be prevented. Ruth Wacuka also states that it is the responsibility of communities to keep children within their circle (Bekele-Piper, 2019). NGOs engage in efforts closing orphanages around the world (Guiney, 2015), in close work with world governments. It is a process, and orphanages cannot be closed from one day to the other as it would leave vulnerable children stranded on the street, being at further risk for sexual exploitation and trafficking. Organizations try and reunite children with their parents, and many are heartbroken and had no idea what was happening to their children. Orphanages still in operation should be staffed with professional personnel with enough workforce for the number of children present. Visitors should not be allowed unless registered in advanced and in very low quantities, with no tourists. Orphanages should follow and reinforce child protection guidelines. Orphanages should not be a tourist attraction. As Becker in the book Learning Services (Bennett et al. 2019) states: "Volunteering with children might seem it's not a big deal, if you, as one sole person, visit an orphanage to help for a few days, but it's the collective impact of that happening over and over again that is causing harm and the only way to stop the trend is to stop individual actions"

## 4. Sustainable Volunteering

Based on warnings from watchdog organizations and key opinion leaders about volunteering directly with children, some providers have ended the work with orphanages or distanced themselves from volunteer tourism all together. TUI Group, Germany's largest travel company, has signed a specialized child protection code, called "The Code" and has ended their relationship with two volunteer tourism operations (Nachhaltigkeitsbericht, 2018; Stitt, 2011). Project Abroad, a major volunteer provider, announced in 2017 that they stopped sending volunteers to orphanages (Knaus, 2017). The network "ReThink Orphanages", formed by major child protection organizations, has dedicated their work entirely to stop the institutionalization of children with a special focus on volunteer tourism. The non-profit organization Forget Me Not is one of the founding members of "ReThinkOrphanages" and dedicates their work to ending child trafficking, closing down orphanages, helping children to reunite with their families and helping poor families to provide an education to their children. But as seen with the advertisement of Go Overseas, there are still many organizations out there that work with orphanages. One of the main contributors worldwide for the funding of orphanages are churches (Knaus, 2017). Hence, it is not solely the travel industry but a combination of many organizations. By analyzing the website of Project Abroad today, they now call their projects "childcare", since the word orphanage tourism has had so much bad media attention. But the truth is that work in orphanages as well as general work with children should be very regulated and criminal background checks should be a standard requirement for volunteers to go abroad. The work should be supervised by local and professional trained staff. Hence, even though some positive developments have occurred, providers are still using the system and children as a tourism commodity.

Volunteer tourism also has many impacts on communities as a whole. There are both positive and negative impacts and sometimes the line between the two is very thin. On one hand, volunteer tourism can take jobs from local people by replacing real jobs with placements for volunteers that do not need to get paid. On the other hand, local receiving organizations need staff to help run the volunteer programs, and volunteers spending money in communities can stimulate the local economy and consequently create jobs. On one hand, it can enhance a local organization with additional resources through knowledgeable volunteers working for free, but it can also waste the resources of organizations as volunteers create additional work, because training volunteers can be time consuming. It can create financial dependency on foreign providers, which makes them vulnerable when providers decide to end the business with local organizations, but it can also give additional funds that are much needed to enhance the work of the organization. Cultural exchange can be encouraged, especially by volunteers staying in local host families. However, volunteers dressing or behaving in an inappropriate way that goes against local values can also paint bad images on foreigners. To ensure sustainable impacts everyone in the supply chain needs to be involved and thoroughly analyze the situation to make the right decisions.

As Bennett et al. (2019) describe, volunteers can bring in new ideas, perspectives and needed skills. Well prepared volunteers with expertise in a special field can have positive impacts on local communities. The problem, as Wearing, Beirman & Grabowski (2020) state, is the top-down approach. Volunteers come in and think they can help the communities without being willing to first learn about their needs.

Volunteering needs to be strategically planned. Long-term approaches are needed and not the band-aid approach, as Bennett et al. (2019) states. A band-aid will help in the short-term but will not solve the root causes to the problem. Lediard (2016) confirms the focus in volunteer tourism is on the micro instead of the macro change. Poverty is a systematic problem and sustainable impact can only be made through advocacy or transformation in the structures of oppression (Lediard, 2016). The community should have a voice in volunteer tourism and be consulted for their needs. To have sustainable impacts through volunteer tourism, the volunteer should be well prepared through previous work experience, an expertise in their field of work, prepared for the cultural differences and the potential poverty awaiting them. The work should be ethical by benefitting the communities and their needs (Wakeford, Orams, 2019).

Community consultation is key and can be done through grass roots involvement such as town hall meetings, where needs of the community can be discussed. It is important to schedule these meetings in locations and at times that are suitable for the various members of the community. Special consideration should be given to give voice to women and other marginalized groups. If necessary, language translation might be used. Once important community needs have been identified, the tour operator, along with local agents can decide how to assist the community. This might mean that depending on budgetary constraints, one group of volunteers might not see the final outcome of the project they are contributing to, instead several groups over a period of time each contribute pieces monetarily or via actual acts of engagement. This ethical approach of putting the community over tourist desires such as to see the impacts of their work, might also mean that monetary contributions could be more beneficial than actual work projects done by volunteers. It is the authors personal experience that when travelers are told about their contribution to a particular project, they are more than happy to forego seeing the final results immediately, knowing that they are ethically contributing to community improvement.

## 5.  Resources and Recommendations

As previously identified the motivation and research of the volunteer is essential for the impact of its work (Heckscher, 2019). In order to identify the motivation, the book "Learning Service the Essential Guide to Volunteering Abroad" (2019) has come up with important questions volunteers should ask themselves:

- What kind of personal growth opportunities do I seek?

- What are my core skills?

- What are my learning goals?

- What are my passions?

- What are my values?

- How does a sense of responsibility or guilt play into my decision?

- What impact do I want to have on the world?

- How does this fit into the "big picture" of my career path or life goals?

It is important that volunteers are honest with themselves and are realistic about these questions. Learning Services states it is vital to see the volunteering experience as a learning experience. Volunteers must be open minded and go abroad with the approach of learning from the communities. It is vital for volunteers to ask the providers the right questions about the work onsite, the local partner they work with (if not getting in touch with grass roots organizations directly) and asking about the funds and where they go. They should look out for a proper selection process that includes a skills-based interview, ideally with references of work experience, former employers or teachers, and a criminal background check. From the information stated above, it is clear that there should be no volunteering done in orphanages. As Becker (Bennett et al., 2019) says "If the orphanage is legitimate, they will not let you just walk in and volunteer". However, even teaching children should only be done if the volunteer has the skills for it and if the work is supervised by professional staff. A volunteer should under no circumstances just be left alone with children, no matter the reason. There are a lot of resources out there that enables volunteers to get a better understanding of the industry and what to look out for:

- Learning Services the essential guide to volunteering abroad: This book was published in 2019 and has an extensive amount of information for volunteers to read and make a sustainable choice for their volunteering.

- Responsible-Volunteering: A website that brings more transparency to the volunteer industry with published articles to many different topics, a small quiz "to check your choice" and other resources needed, before making a decision. www.responsible-voluneering.com.

- #Helpingnothelping: A website that informs volunteers that want to help children, how to go about it. It has additional resources and links to videos that are helpful. https://www.helpingnothelping.org/advice

- The love you give: Watch a short film with the voices of former volunteers that explain the issue with orphanage tourism. http://www.loveyougive.org/

Useful websites, like the ones below are good for volunteers and travelers abroad witnessing human trafficking or sexual exploitation of children. Independent from volunteers working on projects unrelated to children, human trafficking can be witnessed while lying on the beach enjoying the sun, or in a hotel or restaurant.

- Global Modern Slavery: This is a website that lists worldwide local organizations in many countries around the world that work against human trafficking. For volunteers and travelers that witness human trafficking, this might be a good way to look up a local organization to turn to get help. https://www.globalmodernslavery.org/

- Don't look away: A website started by a child protection organization, this website encourages tourists and volunteers to not look away and be aware of their surroundings when travelling in countries with high sexual exploitation of children. This website has information and resources on how to report about child trafficking and sexual exploitation. https://dontlookaway.report/

**Resources for Schools and Universities**

Since volunteers are usually young students, schools and universities play an important role (APEC Tourism Working Group, 2018). It is important for schools and universities that engage in volunteering experiences to educate students properly on the right approaches.

- Orphanage tourism & volunteering a practical resources for schools: This is a whole program designed for students in 10th grade to educate about volunteer tourism and orphanages. This can be downloaded for free: https://issuu.com/weareworldchallenge/docs/orphanage_tourism___volunteering_-_

- ReThink Orphanages: This website has a whole section for schools and universities informing about the dos's and don'ts. https://rethinkorphanages.org

# 6. Four Takeaways from this Chapter

## Be Open Minded and Willing to Learn

When deciding to volunteer it is important to keep an open mind and not think that this trip will change the world. Primarily, this experience will change the volunteer more than anyone else involved. For a positive experience, the volunteer should be open to learn and willing to accept different opinions. Many volunteers come with a preset mind of thinking they will make a real difference and help poor communities. In reality, this experience will teach the volunteer about cultural difference, about local communities and the needs they have and about different values. These needs and values might be very different from what the volunteer initially expected. Closed minded volunteers will have a hard time adapting to these different mind-sets and might get upset that their work onsite might not have as big of an impact as they thought.

## Do Your Research

In order to make sure the volunteering has a sustainable impact; it is very important that each volunteer is doing thorough research. As discussed in this chapter, the majority of providers that come up on a first Google research, might not be the most sustainable ones. Each volunteer should be allowed to ask as many questions as needed and should receive detailed answers by providers. If the providers are not fully transparent, the sustainability can be questioned. Through groups on social media, volunteers can find unbiased reviews and comments to different programs. Many official review platforms are owned by commercial providers themselves and therefore only have positive comments and are biased. Since every volunteer has individual needs and skills, no website or book should be recommending the place to go to. Every volunteer carries the responsibility to do their own research based on their individual skills.

## Do Not Volunteer Directly with Children

No sustainable volunteer provider should be allowing a volunteer to work directly with children, without any supervision or any skills. Supporting a teacher in a school or supporting a primary caretaker in a daycare could be an appropriate work, if the volunteer has educational skills and there was a proper selection process in place. This includes a criminal background check, proper preparation courses and close supervision during the work itself. No volunteer should ever be allowed to work in an orphanage or in a project where they are left alone with the children. This would not be a sustainable project.

## Volunteering Can Be a Life Changing Experience

With the willingness to learn, the right research, asking the right questions and selecting a project that supports your values, volunteering can be a life changing experience. It can create a completely different perspective to the world the volunteer has previously been in. It can influence the volunteer's mindset for future job selections and enforce the good intentions to bring positive change. Even through bad experiences while volunteering, such as questioning the sustainability of the selected project, it can create positive change. Volunteers come back and inform other volunteers about their experience and not to make the same mistakes.

# REFERENCES

Baker, B. (2018). *International Volunteer HQ in Taranaki gets investment from across the ditch.* Retrieved from https://www.stuff.co.nz/business/small-business/100432776/international-volunteer-hq-in-taranaki-gets-investment-from-across-the-ditch

Bekele-Piper, L. (Producer). (2019, November 14). Good Intentions Aren't Enough: Ending Orphanage Tourism [Audio podcast]. Retrieved from https://www.listennotes.com/podcasts/uproot-the-podcast/good-intentions-arent-enough-gHUy5mwFhKC/

Bennett, C., Collins, J., Heckscher, Z. & Papi-Thornton, D. (2018). *Learning Service, The Essential Guide to Volunteering Abroad.* Dorset, England: Red Press Ltd.

Butcher, J. & Smith, P. (2015). Volunteer tourism: The lifestyle politics of international development. *Volunteer Tourism,* 75 – 88. doi: 10.4324/9781315796376-5

Callanan, M. & Thomas, S. (2005). *Volunteer tourism: deconstructing volunteer activities within a dynamic environment.* In Novelli, M. (ed.). *Niche Tourism: Contemporary Issues, Trends and Cases* pp. 183–200. Oxford, UK: Butterworth-Heinemann.

Cheer, J.M. (2019). Introduction. In Cheer, J. M., Mathews L., van Doore, K.E., Flanagan, K. *Modern Day Slavery and Orphanage Tourism* pp. xxiii-xlix. Oxfordshire: CABI.

Coghlan, A., & Weiler, B. (2015). Examining transformative processes in volunteer tourism. Current Issues in Tourism, 1368-3500. doi: 10.1080/13683500.2015.1102209

Comhlamh and the volunteering and orphanages working group (2019). *Children First.* Retrieved from https://www.state.gov/wp-content/uploads/2019/06/2019-Trafficking-in-Persons-Report.pdf

Craft. (2020). *STA Travel revenue.* Retrieved from https://craft.co/sta-travel/revenue

Czarnecki, D. (2018). Voluntourism How to better protect children in destination countries. Retrieved from https://www.responsible-volunteering.com/2018/05/child-protection/

Drobner, S. (2016). *Local implementation of int. volunteer travel programs outsourcing to grass-root organizations.* Retrieved from: https://www.responsible-volunteering.com/2016/10/voluntourism-companies-outsourcing/

Drobner, S. (2018). *IVHQ Review the Capitalization of the Volunteer Sector.* Retrieved from https://www.responsible-volunteering.com/2018/01/ivhq-review-big-business/

Foller-Carroll, A. & Charlebois, S. (2015). The attitudes of students and young professionals toward VolunTourism: a study abroad perspective. *International Journal of Culture, Tourism and Hospitality Research* vol. 10 no. 2, pp. 138 – 160. doi: 10.1108/IJCTHR-04-2015-0027

Foreign Correspondent. (2020). *A trade in Fake Orphans is being driven by western donations.* Retrieved from https://www.youtube.com/watch?time_continue=65&v=lcIsQAqvgcs&feature=emb_logo

Francis, D. & Yasué, M. (2019). A mixed-methods study on the values and motivations of voluntourists. *Tourism Recreation Research.* DOI: 10.1080/02508281.2019.1594574

Gil-Lacruz, A. I., Marcuello, C., Saz-Gil, I. (2018). Gender differences in European volunteer rates. Journal of Gender Studies. doi: 10.1080/09589236.2018.1441016

Guiney, T. (2018). "Hug-an-orphan vacations": "Love" and emotion in orphanage tourism. *The Geographical Journal,* 184: 125-137. doi: 10.1111/geoj.12218

Guiney, T. & Mostafanezhad, M. (2015). The political economy of orphanage tourism in Cambodia. *Tourism Studies,* 15(2), pp. 132 – 155. doi: 10.1177/1468797614563387

Guttentag, D. (2009). The Possible Negative Impacts of Volunteer Tourism. *International Journal of Tourism Research,* 11, 537 – 551. doi: 10.1002/jtr.727

Helping not helping. *MDRC*: Helpful Advice. Retrieved from https://www.helpingnothelping.org/advice

Hertwig, F., Jaeger, L., Koehrer, E., Kosche, M., Mauerer, M., Monshausen, A., & Pluess, C. (2015). *From Volunteering to Voluntourism* (Rev. ed.). Berlin, Germany: Brot fuer die Welt Protestant Agency for Diakonie and Development.

Knaus, C. (2017). *Volunteering company cuts ties to overseas orphanages over child-trafficking fears.* Retrieved from https://www.theguardian.com/world/2017/nov/08/volunteering-company-cuts-ties-to-overseas-orphanages-over-child-trafficking-fears

Lediard, D. (2016). Host Community Narratives of Volunteer Tourism in Ghana: From Developmentalism to Social Justice. *Theses and Dissertations (Comprehensive).* Retrieved from http://scholars.wlu.ca/etd/1862

McKeon, A., Larsson, C., Papi, D., Bylander, M. (2014). *International Volunteering: Trends and Insights.* Better Volunteering Better Care.

Mostafanezhad, M. (2014). Volunteer tourism and the popular humanitarian gaze. *Geoforum,* 54, pp. 111 – 118. Retrieved from https://doi.org/10.1016/j.geoforum.2014.04.004

Nahill, B. (2018). *How to be a Responsible Turtle Volunteer.* Retrieved from https://www.responsible-volunteering.com/2018/10/responsible-turtle-volunteer/

Pariyar, S. (2017). Annual $173 Billion Worth of Volunteer Tourism Industry Is Enough To Make A Change. Retrieved from https://thriveglobal.com/stories/annual-173-billion-worth-of-volunteer-tourism-industry-is-enough-to-make-a-change/

ReThink Orphanages (2018). *ReThink Orphanages United States.* Retrieved from https://us.rethinkorphanages.org/

Sin, H. L., Oakes, T. & Mostafanezhad, M. (2015). Traveling for a cause: Critical examinations of volunteer tourism and social justice. *Tourism Studies,* vol. 15(2) 119-131. doi: 10.1177/1468797614563380

Start the Adventure (2020). Make a REAL difference in Cambodia with Love Volunteers! (2020). *Go Overseas.* Retrieved from https://www.gooverseas.com/volunteer-abroad/cambodia/love-volunteers/22202.

Stitt, D. (2011). Why we started Gap 360. Retrieved from https://blog.gap360.com/why-we-startedgap360/?fbclid=IwAR1UYDKn15zl9D52IUHenALoaqRE_MM1U5cT9Nhtf46ouHC0XTDQnNVnskQ

The Love you Give (2019). *The Love You Give the untold story of orphanages.* Retrieved from http://www.loveyougive.org/#about

Trafficking in persons report. (2019). *United States Department of State Publication.* Retrieved from: https://www.state.gov/wp-content/uploads/2019/06/2019-Trafficking-in-Persons-Report.pdf

Trihas, N., Antonaki, M. and Kouremenou, A. (2014). Beyond Sea, Sun and Sand: Volunteer Tourism as an Emerging Alternative Form of Tourism in Greece. International Conference "Cross-Cultural Issues in Tourism & Hospitality", 14-16 May, Chania, Crete, Greece.

TUIGroup. (2018). *Nachhaltigkeitsbericht.* Retrieved from https://www.tuigroup.com/damfiles/default/tuigroup15/de/nachhaltigkeit/berichterstattung-downloads/2019/nachhaltigkeitsbericht-de-en/TUI_CSR18_DE.pdf-d4d29ec3e01512f8a810997c1795991e.pdf?fbclid=IwAR0bfu8lgkDtemsRyVVKvdJ0BWKGjEyzAM-laQ5VCYIUGEjvNvtMd9mSsYg

UNICEF. (2011). *With the Best Intentions: A Study of Attitudes towards Residential Care in Cambodia.* Phnom Penh, Cambodia: UNICEF Cambodia.

United Nations. (2010). *General Assembly Sixty-fourth Session Agenda item 64.* Retrieved from https://www.unicef.org/protection/alternative_care_Guidelines-English.pdf

United States Government Action Plan on Children in Adversity. (2012). *A Framework for international Assistance: 2012-2-17.* Retrieved from https://www.childreninadversity.gov/docs/default-source/default-document-library/apca.pdf?sfvrsn=2

U.S Department of State Office to Monitor and Combat Trafficking in Persons (2018). *Trafficking in Persons Report.* Retrieved from https://www.state.gov/wp-content/uploads/2019/01/282798.pdf

Wearing, S., Beirman, D. & Grabowski, S. (2020). *Engaging volunteer tourism in post-disaster recovery in Nepal.* Annals of Tourism Research, Elsevier, vol. 80(C). Retrieved from https://doi.org/10.1016/j.annals.2019.102802

Wearing, S. & McGehee, N. G. (2013). *International Volunteer Tourism Integrating Travellers and Communities.* Oxfordshire, UK: CABI.

Westendorp, L. & Hofstee, T. (2017). *Orphanage Tourism: Report on a Survey conducted in the Netherlands.* Leiden, Netherlands: Better Care Network Netherlands.

Wilkinson, B., McCool, J. & Bois, G. (2014). Voluntourism: an analysis of the online marketing of afast-growing industry. *The International Journal of Communication and Health,* no. 4, pp. 10 – 15. Retrieved from http://communicationandhealth.ro/upload/number4/WILKINSON-MCCOOL-BOIS.pdf

Chapter 6

# Applied Ecolodge Research: Creating Cultural Context Through a "Continuity of the Vernacular" Planning and Design Approach

*Hitesh Mehta*
*FRIBA FASLA FAAK*
*Associate AIA*

## Abstract

*Al Gore's "Inconvenient Truth" followed by other documentaries like Leonardo de Caprio's "11ᵗʰ Hour" and Louie Psihoyos's "The Cove" graphically brought to light the dangers of global warming, threat to planet ecosystems, food famines, unsustainable homocentric approaches etc. to many people in the tourism and travel industry and the resultant awareness has created a 'tipping point' amongst the main financial decision makers where those people who acknowledge the importance of sustainability and are doing something about it, is outnumbering those who do not. Now, more than ever, the hospitality industry has recognized that environmental and social stewardship are good for business, good for the planet, and are vital to the future of travel and tourism. We have also reached a tipping point whereby the global traditional hospitality industry is more widely accepting sustainable tourism. The future of sustainability is indeed good. The COVID 19 crisis offers a chance for restructuring and better alignment with environmental or social values when tourism comes back. With greater appreciation for nature now, this crisis also offers an opportunity to include more knowledge on what makes people and destinations resilient, happy, and well.*

*This paper makes the case for a culturally appropriate Ecolodge Landscape and Building Design. It dwells into how research can be applied in lodge design to create authentic "continuity of the vernacular" experiences. This paper will address the close relationship between ecolodges and surrounding cultural landscapes and explore the role that site planning and design plays in this regard. And what does an 'authentic' accommodation look like? How does it differ from conventional accommodation? How can we create lodges that are aesthetically sustainable? How can we create a lodge architecture that is timeless? An applied-research case-study of a "continuity of the vernacular architecture" project will be presented illustratively to show how cultural context is created during ecolodge planning and design.*

**Keywords:** Ecolodges, Vernacular Architecture, Cultural Context, Continuity of the Vernacular, Applied Research.

# 1. Introduction

Most of the modern design introduced by the majority of architects and landscape architects is lacking in cultural context and sense of place. Unfortunately, very few contemporary buildings are environmentally and socially conscious (Sustainability Leaders Project, 2017). Many of these buildings stand out like sore thumbs and look out of place in their rich cultural surroundings. Neither are they timeless. One must look at the Beijing Olympics Architectural buildings such as Birds Nest and you realize the large amounts of resource depleting materials that were used to build these 'white-elephant' buildings (www.npr.org, 2012).

Especially in hospitality design, it is time for 'developing countries' to stop looking at foreign designers and inspirations for their buildings and instead use local architects and designers to create an architectural language that is a "continuity of the vernacular" of the respective cultural landscape. It is time that these countries and developers recognize the skills of their own professionals and wisdom of local peoples. Only if the relevant skill or experience is not available locally should the developer search beyond the borders. And if there is no choice but to have international consultants, developers should always have local consultants on the team to provide much needed local wisdom and experience.

It is in the field of hospitality in rural areas that the contrast between modern design and the respective landscape is greatest. Conventionally designed buildings always seem to feel out of place in their rich cultural landscapes. It is in this regards that ecolodges stand on their own.

The role design plays in Ecolodges is that it provides context and conveys a sense of "isolation" and "wilderness" of being away from the negative visual impacts of modern civilization glass, steel, concrete and aluminum facades, a common aesthetic of conventional accommodations. Ecolodges are as authentic as accommodations can get in the tourism industry. They are indeed the environmentally and socially friendly tourist accommodation components of Ecotourism and by their definition, can only be found in natural locations and not urban areas. As such, the design of an authentic ecolodge encourages close interaction with the natural and cultural environment and has an atmosphere that is appropriate to the site's specific setting. It is this metaphysical 'sense of place' that is one of the key ingredients in distinguishing ecolodges from conventional accommodations (Russel et al., 1995). Unlike conventional accommodations, they provide a spiritual communion with nature and culture.

After seven years of research, feedback from stakeholders in the ecotourism industry (International Ecolodge Forum 2, 1995), interviews with architects and professors, eco-consultants, developers, operators, many indigenous communities, The International Ecotourism Society developed the following criteria (Mehta H. et al, 2002) to determine visual authenticity in Ecolodges:

1.  The lodge needs to fit into its specific physical and cultural context through careful attention to form, landscaping, and color as well as using vernacular architecture.

2.  The buildings and plantings need to have minimal visual and physical impact on the natural surroundings and utilize traditional building techniques during construction.

3.  Both the architecture and landscape design need to use locally available and environmentally friendly building and furnishings materials.

4.  Collaborate with the local community, including community members, wherever possible, in the initial physical planning and design stages of construction.

The most important stakeholders in an ecotourism project are not the investors, government agencies or project owners, but the local communities, who should be involved in the project planning right from the beginning. This means involving the community in project decisions and using local contractors, consultants, and labor throughout the project. Training local people on the various aspects of planning, designing, construction and operations is a vital component of a successful ecolodge.

An ecolodge is considered in context with its cultural landscape if its planning and design borrows from the design principles practiced on the vernacular architecture and if it employs local construction techniques and materials (Aysan, 1988). This 'continuity of the vernacular' approach to planning and design will, aesthetically, provide an architectural style that will be timeless.

## 2.  Definitions, Principles and Criteria

### Ecotourism

Ecotourism is any tourism in nature-based locations which practices the three main principles of: protection of nature; benefits to local people and offering of interpretative programs.

Ecotourism is responsible travel to natural areas that conserves the environment, sustains the well-being of the local people, and creates knowledge and understanding through interpretation and education of all involved (visitors, staff and the visited)" (GEN, 2018).

Ecotourism is an established global niche market in which traveler's vacation at sustainably designed accommodations, called Ecolodges, where they can marvel at pristine and often fragile natural habitats. But delivering such ecofriendly travel destinations requires project owners to find a delicate balance between financial, social, and environmental goals.

Ecotourism Destination Planning's main premise is that a planner should enhance the environment, not take away from it. If you plan a road or trail in a wildlife refuge that disrupts a migration path, or site a property in a rain forest that requires removing trees, the planner is taking away from the land.

If not executed properly, Ecotourism projects run the risk of destroying the same pristine destinations that tourists have come to visit. Delivering ecotourism's planned environmental benefits is not always easy. One of the biggest obstacles are project owners who like the idea of ecotourism but start to lose interest when they must make tough decisions to balance cost against environmental goals. The loss of biodiversity and wildlife habitats, the production of waste and polluted effluent in areas that have little or no capacity to absorb them are just some of the worries. (Epler-Wood, M., 2002)

## Ecolodges

Since the term ecolodges emerged in the early 1990's, there has been several interpretations by various ecotourism organizations and using different criteria systems to evaluate accommodation facilities. Ecolodges are the environmentally and socially friendly tourist accommodation components of Ecotourism. By their definition, you can only find Ecolodges in natural locations and not in cities and towns.

Global tourists, consciously choosing ecolodges, expect from their travel, four main things:

    a) That part of their money is going towards the conservation of neighboring environments

    b) That part of their money is going towards helping benefit local communities

    c) That they will be getting a rich, memorable interpretive experiences

    d) That they will experience a "spiritual communion with Nature and /or culture.

The design of an ecolodge and the activities provided within the facility should encourage close interaction with the natural and cultural environment and have an atmosphere that is appropriate to the site's specific setting. Some examples include Cree Village Ecolodge's harmony with its First Nations cultural setting in Northern Canada; Adrère Amellal Ecolodge's setting in a Desert oasis, Egypt and Crosswaters Ecolodge and Spa's siting in the bamboo montane forests of South China (Mehta, H., 2010). It is this metaphysical 'sense of place' created by each of the above-mentioned lodges "continuity of the vernacular' architecture, that is one of the key ingredients in distinguishing ecolodges from traditional hotels. It should be noted that right from the early days, ecolodges were looked upon as those that MUST be designed in harmony with the local natural and cultural environment, using the principles of sustainable design (Hawkins, et al., 1995).

Ecolodge Design is a conscientious and creative approach, whereby:

- A designer is egoless and who practices a holistic approach to design.

- A designer encourages integrated and participatory approaches in the design process and one who recognizes local knowledge and uses it wisely in the design.

- A designer who not only is interested in aesthetics but in the substance a beautiful design, but which is also economically, socially, environmentally, and spiritually sustainable.

Image 1: An example of an Authentic Ecolodge where all the design-based criteria have been utilized

*Source: HM Design*

The author felt the need in 1999 to focus on the principles that constitute an ecolodge because it is the basic principles that differentiate ecolodges from traditional nature lodges and hotels. Ten basic principles that constitute an ecolodge were discussed in a research paper and presented at an international conference in Malaysia (Mehta, H., 1999). After noticing that these principles were not effective in reducing greenwashing in the lodge industry, this author then took the ten principles, converted them into Criteria and presented in a book (Mehta et al, 2002), a rating system to certify what determines an Ecolodge. Eight years later, this author then added an additional criterion (Mehta. H, 2010) which is related to the involvement, from day one, of local community wisdom and construction skills. This revised rating system was later used to ascertain which Ecolodges featured in the book *Authentic Ecolodges* (2010).

## Knowledge Box: What is an Ecolodge?

---

AUTHENTIC ECOLODGE CRITERIA:

For a lodge to be considered an Authentic Ecolodge, it needs to satisfy only five of the eleven criteria. First and foremost, an Authentic Ecolodge **MUST** embody the three main criteria of ecotourism:

1. nature must be protected and conserved
2. through community outreach and education programs, local community must benefit
3. interpretive programs must be offered to educate both tourist and employees about the surrounding natural and cultural environments.

Following these 'must' criteria, then, an ecolodge must satisfy two additional criteria from this below list of eight:

1. Fit into its specific physical and cultural contexts through careful attention to form, landscaping, and color as well as using vernacular architecture.
2. Use environmentally friendly building and furnishings materials.
3. Have minimal impact on the natural surroundings and utilize traditional building techniques during construction.
4. Endeavor to work with the local community, including community members, wherever possible, in the initial physical planning and design stages of construction.
5. Use alternative and sustainable means of water acquisition and at the same time reduce overall water consumption.
6. Meet its energy needs through passive design and renewable sources.
7. Provide for careful handling (reduce, refuse, recycle, reuse) and disposal of solid waste.
8. Use environmentally friendly sewage treatment systems.

Authentic Ecolodges (2010)

---

It was not until 2007 that this author, defined Ecolodges as *"low-impact, nature-based accommodations of two to seventy-five rooms that protect the surrounding environment; benefit the local community; offer tourists an interpretative and interactive participatory experience; provide a spiritual communion with nature and culture and are designed, constructed and operated in an environmentally and socially sensitive manner."* (Mehta, H., 2007).

## 3. The Case for Cultural Context in Ecolodge Landscape Architecture and Building Design

Architectural style is a medium for the promotion of cultural identities and cohesion. The overarching emphasis of this study is that throughout history, architecture has been creatively adopted to the need of its users and the characteristics of its climate and location. It has always fulfilled the needs and nourished the spirit of its people, promoting cultural cohesion even today. In this context, it is crucial to explore traditional techniques of vernacular architecture in ecolodges. The common thread linking vernacular architecture, with present day ecolodges, is in the application of sustainable building practices using intelligent building forms, fabric, and orientation.

The philosophy of contextualism is truly relevant in ecolodge planning and design each site requiring its own approach depending on the cultural, climate and physical setting. An ecolodge should demonstrate the same level of sensitivity to the cultural context as it does to the physical context. The design of the facility should be congruous with the cultural environment in which it operates, incorporating cultural motifs and traditional styles of vernacular architecture wherever possible. The use of vernacular architectural principles in the design will allow the facility to reflect the local cultural history, and be visually and culturally sustainable over time.

And each cultural region also demands a different approach since there can be many different cultural architectural styles within a country. So, an ecolodge in the Kikuyu country on the rainforest slopes of Mount Kenya would be different from an ecolodge in the desert landscape of Rendille peoples in Northern Kenya. In respect to local cultural traditions, for example in Islamic regions, there is a need to design ecolodges with a more gradual transition from public through semi-public & semi-private to private. Design layouts and details should conform to Islamic cultural traditions. For example, in consideration of most of the guests at the desert ecolodges in Saudi Arabia, orientation to Mecca should be built into the various elements of the ecolodge. Local design styles (e.g., Najd etc.) should also be respected. Saudi attitudes to the family, women, bachelors etc. should also be respected and therefore spatial privacy is an important concept for a Desert Ecolodge. Saudi appreciation of the desert, its beauty and its wildlife must be considered when planning a desert ecolodge.

The use of an area's vernacular architecture helps assimilate ecolodges into the local cultural context, and here they can serve two additional roles: First, they can help reduce any feelings of cultural intrusion that may be felt toward the ecolodge by local traditional peoples. Secondly, if they are done well, they can enhance the tourists' experience and appreciation of the local cultural forms and styles. As a building style, vernacular architecture represents the social and cultural norms of specific communities and their environment (Aysan, 1988).

## Vernacular Architecture and Traditional Ecological Knowledge:

Bernard Rudofsky (1964) stated that during his time, non-pedigreed architecture was little known and did not have a name for it. For want of generic label, he called it vernacular, anonymous, spontaneous, rural, as the case may have been. Vernacular Architecture is a built form resulting from the forces of society, forces of technology and forces due to physical environment. The built form is a response to the needs of a given society. Vernacular architecture is '*the architecture of people*' (Paul Oliver 2005). It is related to the cultural context and available resources, is customarily owner or community built, and utilizing traditional technologies and local materials. All forms of vernacular architecture are built to meet specific needs, economies, accommodating the values, and ways of life of the cultures that produce them *(Philokyprou, M, 2015)*.

Vernacular building tradition means the local wisdom, beliefs, customs, ways of life and practices are handed down from generation to generation, all related to building. These include the selection of location, process of design of the house, preparation of local materials, community-help in building the house, maintenance, repairs when it is damaged, and extending the house when the number of family member increases (P Nimsamer and N, Walliman, 2014). Thus, the social organization and level of technical know-how of a given society, plus the climate of the zone of settlement and the materials available within this zone determine the society's-built form, that is, vernacular architecture (Anyamba T.C. and Adebayo A.A, 1993).

Ecological anthropologists, ethnobiologists, conservation biologists, other scholars, and the pharmaceutical industry all share an interest in traditional knowledge for social, scientific or economic reasons (Berkes F, Colding J, FolkeSource C, 2000). For Planners and Architects, '*Traditional Ecological Knowledge*' is of great importance in learning about local typology of Architectural forms and spatial relationships. '*Traditional Ecological Knowledge*' (TEK) refers to the *"evolving knowledge acquired by indigenous and local peoples over hundreds or thousands of years through direct contact with the environment "*(Berkes F, 1999).

For Indigenous peoples, TEK that is conveyed through mythology forms the foundation of a complex understanding of the natural world. This knowledge is specific to a location and includes the relationships between plants, animals, natural phenomena, landscapes, and timing of events that are used for lifeways, including but not limited to hunting, fishing, trapping, agriculture, and forestry. TEK is an accumulating body of knowledge, practice, and belief, evolving by adaptive processes and handed down through generations by cultural transmission. It is also about the relationship of human and non-human living beings with one another and with the environment. It encompasses the world view of indigenous people which includes human and animal relationships, spirituality, ecology, and more. (US Fish and Wildlife Service, 2011)

Growing interest in traditional knowledge since the 1980s is indicative of the need to gain further insights into indigenous and/or local practices of resource use from an ecological perspective, which is one of the objectives of this paper.

In recent years, there has been a strong avocation for Lo-TEK, a catalogue of sustainable, adaptable, and resilient technologies that are borne out of necessity. In contrast to modern high-tech construction, Lo-TEK is an indigenous infrastructure that expands the definitions of modern technology. It is local, hand-made, inexpensive, and easily constructed soft system, embedded with traditional ecological knowledge, practices and beliefs (Watson, J. 2019).

Lo-TEK explores the intersection of design and radical indigenism. Coined by Princeton Professor and Cherokee Nation citizen Eva Marie Garroute, radial indigenism argues for a *"rebuilding of knowledge and explores indigenous philosophies capable of generating new dialogues"* (Garroute, E. 2006).

**Knowledge Box**

> Lo-TEK:
> A design movement to rebuild an understanding of indigenous philosophy and vernacular architecture that generates sustainable, climate resilient infrastructure. (Watson, J 2019)

**Continuity of the Vernacular:**

The Declaration of Amsterdam underlines the necessity of continuity of existing social and physical realities in urban and rural communities (European Architectural Heritage, 1975). According to the ICOMOS Charter of Vernacular Architecture, where there is no break in the continuous utilization of vernacular forms, a code of ethics within the community can serve as a tool of intervention (ICOMOS, 1999).

The challenge in Ecolodge Planning and Design is to create a sustainable aesthetic. One that is timeless. A timeless architecture does not become obsolete because its relevance continues by it assuming other functions by the way it was designed. The most difficult aspect of designing for timelessness is the fact that it may take a long period of time for this realization. Throughout history, and even in the present, mostly architecture with a timeless quality has lent itself to spiritual, sacred, and memorial types (Essawy, S., 2017). The construction and layout of such architecture could define the very idea of a timeless architecture. Materials used in the construction are timeless; with every day of sun, rain, freeze, and thaw the stone is stripped of another mask that continuously reveals more and more of its beauty.

In *"The Timeless Way of Building,"* Christopher Alexander presents a new theory of architecture, building, and planning which has at its core that age-old process by which the people of a society have always pulled the order of their world from their own being. Over thousands of years old, vernacular architecture is looks the same today as it has always been. A good example is the Maasai Manyatta's in Eastern Africa. The aesthetic of form and space have sustained through the ages. The great traditional buildings and villages of the past:

> in which the human feels at home, have always been made by people who were very close to the center of this way. It is not possible to make great buildings, or great towns, beautiful places, places where you feel yourself, places where you feel alive, except by following this way Timeless architecture is when buildings and the spaces around it are themselves as ancient in their form, as the trees and hills surrounding the buildings (Alexander, C., 1979).

Vernacular architecture has always been timeless and continuous in architectural development according to space and function since traditional buildings acquired their final form because of extensions and additions to an initially smaller unit to satisfy the temporal requirements of the respective owner. Extensions and renovations and were usually designed on site and were implemented by the user himself or by some craftsmen (Philokyprou, M. 2015).

For Ecolodges, timeless architectural design needs to be built on a strong research foundation. This approach leads to a competitive advantage and client benefits. One just needs to look at the popularity of UNESCO World Heritage Cultural Sites (Tourism Watch, 2018) to see how people are yearning to visit and appreciate vernacular architecture. Since vernacular architecture is the expression of local ethnicity, it is crucial that Ecolodges (a new concept and which have different spatial and volumetric functions than vernacular spaces) borrow from the basic planning and design principles used in vernacular architecture and then create an aesthetic that is a continuity of the vernacular. There is need for continuity so that principles of coherence inform the practice of conservation, which in recent times has led to making 'heritage' a marketable commodity. To develop an effective documentation practice, it is necessary to promote a conservation ethos, which is based on a knowledge base rather than marketing techniques. The most lasting and visible examples of a culture are the buildings which survive our mortal selves. The development and maintenance of built environment is a fundamental homo sapiens activity, which offers an opportunity to engage with culture in an intimate manner (Ganju, M., 2016).

The continuity in vernacular architecture is related to space and time, involves structural, typological, functional, and social issues, and has multiple readings and interpretations. To create ecolodges that are in cultural context with the local communities, it is crucial to have a strong and proven Methodology and Planning/Design process.

**Methodologies and Process:**

The methodology and process employed by planners and architects is crucial in ensuring that ecolodges are in cultural context with their surroundings and exhibit a continuity of the vernacular architecture. After twenty-five years of planning and designing ecolodges, this author has discovered that positive cultural context results are obtained by using the below methodologies and following the proper process. Seven forms of methodology should be used to prepare a Sustainable Conceptual Master Plan and Continuity of the Vernacular Architectural Illustrations:

> Before making a visit to the site it is important to 1) research the history, culture, flora and fauna of the site environs and its surrounding areas; 2) Review existing documents and information on the site, such as market and feasibility study, socio-environmental diagnosis, vegetation study and tree inventory, topography and 3) carry out a pre-site visit AutoCAD/GIS composite site suitability analysis.

The next step would be to carry out a physical on-site research and analysis trip. After meeting with the clients to discuss the development program, the first thing that needs to be done is a participatory meeting with local community to listen to their aspirations, concerns, needs, dreams etc. This first site visit should include ground truthing the information in the Site Survey topography map and the various site suitability analysis drawings. An important component of the on-site analysis is a metaphysical 'six-senses' workshop which helps the site planner understand and immerse into the 'chi' (energy) of the site. The purpose of this workshop is to ensure that the clients, staff and local consultants are provided the opportunity to share their views and sensory connections to the site and region, and in so doing help the planner/architect better understand the site. The site visit should be followed by interviews with the various stakeholders, on-site visits (with local people) to local villages and museums to research and sketch the typology of form of vernacular architecture and artifacts as well as availability of local building materials. Also important during this trip is to visit and study neighboring existing tourism lodges. Architects and Landscape Architects in particular, should visit the main library in the city to research books on the local culture surrounding the ecolodge.

The next step would be to conduct a Participatory Planning Charette that is held on-site and in an enclosed comfortable area. The client, local consultants, marketing and financial feasibility consultant and local community representatives are crucial participants and provided valuable information and critique. The planning charette accelerates the planning process by creating an interactive environment with the client and the consultants working together without the normal interruptions that delay communications. This planning process assists in reviewing program issues, environmental constraints and provides insight into the physical and market potential of the various products. The participatory charette oriented planning and design process is a most effective and efficient means of providing clients and local consultants with a specific work product quickly and comprehensively. This inclusive workshop format provides an early feasibility review of the overall plan with minimal investment of both time and money. The drawings produced in this charette are "Opportunities and Constraints Plan", several Land Use Options and an approved Land Use Plan.

After the consultants return to their offices, the next stage is the preparation of the draft Conceptual Master Plan and for the Planners and Architects, further research on local vernacular architecture. It is after this that the Architectural Concepts are drawn up and Illustrations created. These are then sent to the client for final review. The final step is for the consultants to make the revisions and prepare the Final Conceptual Master Plan.

If the client decides to take the process to the next stage Schematic Plan, planners and architects should conduct another site visit over the course of six-months. This is to ensure that the site is viewed during different weather conditions and to understand in detail, how Traditional Ecological Knowledge has been used in the construction of the local vernacular. The seventh form of methodology is an on-site ground-truthing exercise that should be undertaken to confirm the locations of the various project elements. This enables planners and architects to receive valuable feedback before the preparation of the Schematic Master Plan and Building Architectural Plans.

**Applied Research Process:**

The process of implementing Research in projects should include the following stages:

1.  Compilation of background documentation. Research on culture, vernacular architecture.

2.  Review and analysis of background documentation

3.  Presentation to client

4.  Site visit and reconnaissance.

5.  Research traditional Architectural Forms and spatial relationships. Study local construction techniques.

6.  On-site metaphysical workshop

7.  Planning workshop and charette

8.  Presentation to client

9.  Finalize site analysis

10. Refinement of approved plan and further research

11. Visit Site to carry ground-truthing and analysis of new acquired sites

12. Prepare Revised Land Use Plan

13. Present Land Use Plans to client

14. Prepare FINAL Conceptual Master Plan

15. Create Continuity of the Vernacular Architectural renderings

16. Submission of Final Plan and Renderings to client

## 4.  Applied Research and Best Practice Case Studies

For practicing architects and landscape architects, research can be a difficult concept to pin down and define. It is a term which can mean different things to different designers, but what is clear is that research can be the intellectual fuel for the engine of innovation and growth for many architects' practices. Applied architectural research is putting knowledge gleaned from basic research into use and if time and money permits it, studying its efficacy (Buday, R., 2017).

Compared to the long history of conventional tourist accommodations, ecolodges are a more recent concept and because of this, it is not easy to find an authentic and committed team of eco-consultants who have a good understanding of what it requires to master plan, design and build them. Ecolodge planning and design in this global age of heightened cultural and environmental sensitivity needs to be participatory, holistic in nature and sustainable in all aspects of the planning and design process. Architectural and Landscape Architectural interventions are crucial in creating authentic ecolodge experiences and this approach is lacking in most regions of the world (Sustainability Leaders Project, 2017).

For this paper, we will be looking at one applied research project by the firm EDSA and where this author was the Project Manager Crosswaters Ecolodge and Spa. This project is a celebration of the Bamboo to reflect its context with the surrounding Bamboo Forests. Bamboo is called the "friend of the people" in China because of its diverse use in everything from food and cooking to furniture, paper, musical instruments, boats and houses. Crosswaters Ecolodge and Spa, when it opened to the guests, was the largest project in the world as regards the use of bamboo in a commercial project. It was also the first instance of this method of construction (bamboo as a structural member in a place of habitation) being introduced in Asia in a large project. The spirit of the bamboo is celebrated in Landscape Architecture, Architecture and Interior Design. The bamboo was harvested on the site and is one of the most environmentally friendly building materials in the world.

This paper will look at three important stages of ecolodge planning and design and then showcase Crosswaters for each of the various stages and how the research has been put into use on the ground.

## 4.1 Research and Analysis

Before a Landscape Architect creates a site plan for an ecolodge, he/she needs to conduct an in-depth physical environmental analysis of the chosen site. The main objective of this pre site-visit analysis is to create a Composite Site Suitability Analysis map which identifies the optimum locations of buildings to create the least ecological impact on the site (Business Mirror, 2016)

'Continuity of the vernacular' ecolodges are those that provide guests a spiritual union with the local culture. These projects cater to travelers who want to learn about other places and local people rather than just escape their familiar surroundings but at the same time make a positive difference to the local communities they visit. These unique experiences provide a competitive advantage to project owners. Experience of working in over sixty-five countries around the world has taught this author that one cannot have authentic sustainability if one does not consider the 'spiritual' aspects, also referred to by scientists and philosophers as Metaphysical (Sustainability Leaders Project, May 2017). It should be emphasized that "spiritual" as referred to Ecolodge Planning and Design is not associated with religion but as the energy that is embodied on a site and how as a planner, one can create site plans and architectural designs that not only respect these energies but also enhance them.

Depending on the wishes of the clients, designers should employ respective metaphysical analysis workshops on the site that help all consultants and clients to use their respective six senses to understand and connect at a deeper level to the land. Metaphysical philosophies are being widely practiced in many parts of the world. Of note is the Chinese philosophy of Feng Shui and the Indian Vedic philosophy of Vaastu Shastra. Also, numerous indigenous tribes have a holistic planning philosophy including the First Nations tribes of the Americas and the aboriginal peoples of Australia. All these are ways of living, which depend on the interdependence of humans and nature. Recognizing these ways of life calls for a fundamental shift in the priorities of our culture from a civilization based on endless, unsustainable economic growth at the expense of nature, towards a sustainable world based on ecological principles and respect for both cultural and natural diversity.

To employ various metaphysical analysis, planning and design philosophies and apply these thousands of years of 'research', the Landscape Architect should bring onto the team, a Master (with at least 15 years' experience) or an indigenous elder before any planning or design work is carried out on the project. Tapping local wisdom is crucial to understanding the ancestral planning, design and construction customs and learning about climatic design and how for centuries, local communities have addressed their comfortability through use of orientations, air flows, thick walls etc. It is this research that will lead to an understanding of local Vernacular Architecture.

## *Best Practice Applied Research: Environmental and Social Site Analysis*

The case study used for this paper, Crosswaters Ecolodge and Spa, is in Nankun Shan Nature Reserve, Central Guangdong Province, South China and is 80 miles north-east from Guangzhou, the capital of the province. The reserve was established in 1984, and its major objective is to protect the subtropical evergreen broadleaf forest. The nature reserve lies within the boundaries of the Nankun Shan Forest Park, which covers an area of 100 sq. miles. There are over 1300 plants to be found in the park with over 12 sq. miles of Bamboo. The main species of Bamboo is the Phyllostachys pubescens. There are over 74 bird species in the reserve and nationally protected species include the Mountain Scopes Owl, Grey-headed Woodpecker and Orange-Bellied Leafbird. There are over 176 species of Butterflies with four of them considered near threatened. Over 5,000 people live in the Nature Reserve and it should be noted that the main income generating activity of the local people was the harvesting of Bamboo for use in scaffolding in Guangzhou and Hong Kong. The largest village in the reserve, Shangping Village lies a few miles from the Crosswaters Ecolodge site.

The Landscape Architects began the project, from their home office, by carrying out research on the environmental history of China, as well as on local and regional environmental / social issues. This includes visits to the local Library, bookstore as well as internet.

From the physical topo base contour map provided by the client, the landscape architect used GIS (Geographic Information System) add-ons (Spatial Analyst and 3-D Analyst) to create slope, elevation, slope aspect, vegetation, soil, hydrology and 3-D terrain individual component analysis. This was then followed by individual suitability studies that identified optimal development locations for each analytical category that would have the least impact on the land. For the elevation and hydrology studies, development was limited to areas outside the 100-year flood zone (+/-416m) and 30 meters below the highest elevation. For the slope aspect analysis, ideal locations were facing the south for purposes of Feng Shui. Development on slopes was limited to 2-25% throughout the site. For vegetation analysis, development was focused on previously disturbed areas where the locals had used the land to plant orchards of fruit trees.

Figure 1: Individual Component Environmental Analysis

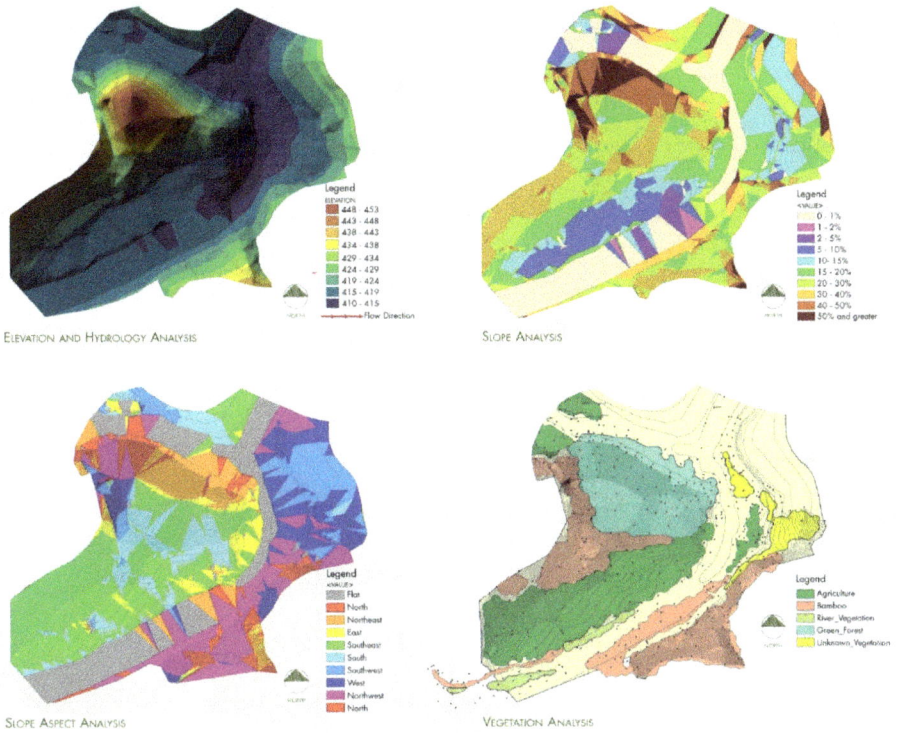

ELEVATION AND HYDROLOGY ANALYSIS

SLOPE ANALYSIS

SLOPE ASPECT ANALYSIS

VEGETATION ANALYSIS

*Source: EDSA*

To gain a true sense of development versus conservation potential, the individual site-suitability analysis drawings are digitally layered to create a Composite Site Suitability Analysis diagram showing areas of prime, secondary and restricted site development potential. The prime areas identify optimum locations for the various buildings, while at the same time, have the least ecological impact. The restricted areas are those that require protection and where there should be no development.

Figure 2: Composite Environmental Analysis

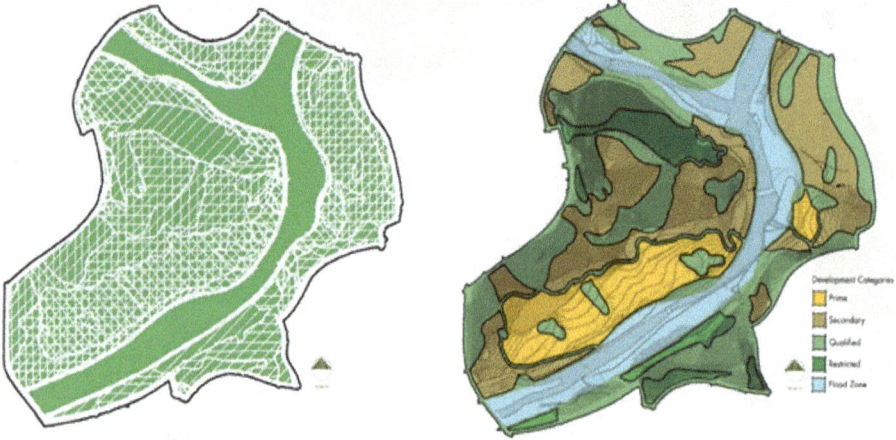

*Source: EDSA*

The Landscape Architect and Architect made three different **on-site visits** (one week each) during winter, spring and summer and spend quality time on the site first understanding and then studying the ways of living of the local minority Chinese people Keija, who make up the majority of the population on the Mountain.

The initial site visit unlocked a rich culture in the surrounding villages. The design team immersed themselves into the community and local government thus winning their trust, which has been crucial to the success of this project. Eager to be included in the planning process, the local people proudly invited the design team into their homes to share their culture. The landscape architects used sketching as a technique to capture the spirit of place (gestalt). They particularly studied Keija vernacular Houses and relationships to gardens and philosophical connections with the Bamboo. The way the building forms relate to each other and to the landscape became important to planning, as well as in the more detailed organization of the buildings from the interior to the exterior. They also looked for clues and responses from what they observed –drainage, existing agriculture, water levels, seasonal visitor traffic, vernacular construction techniques, local crafts industry etc.

Figure 3: Sketching techniques were utilized to capture the "chi' (energy) of the Keija village neighboring Crosswaters Ecolodge. These 'genius loci" studies were part of the initial presentation to clients.

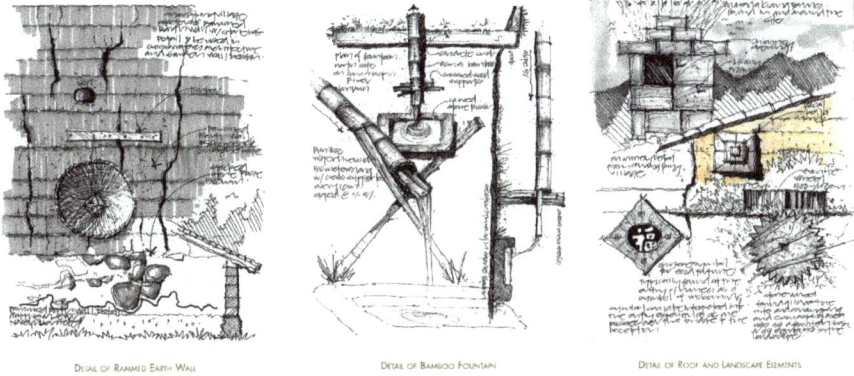

DETAIL OF RAMMED EARTH WALL        DETAIL OF BAMBOO FOUNTAIN        DETAIL OF ROOF AND LANDSCAPE ELEMENTS

*Source: EDSA*

Figure 4: Typology of form studies of authentic Keija Houses showing inside outside and volumetric relationships.

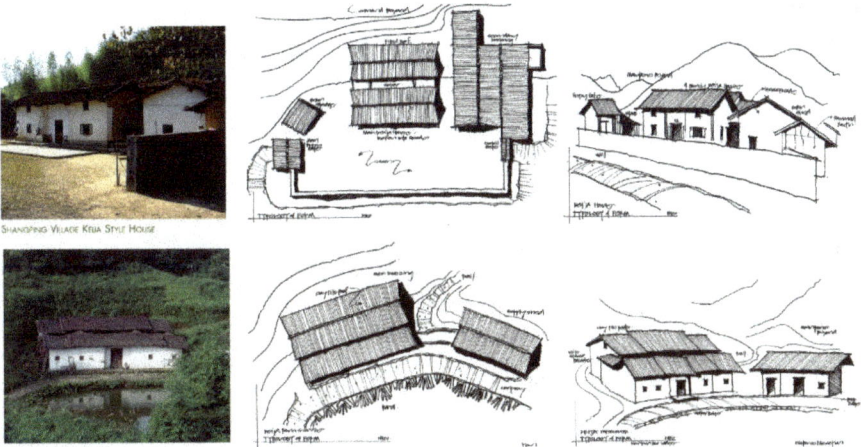

SHANGPING VILLAGE KEIJA STYLE HOUSE

MOUNTAIN VILLAGE HOUSE

*Source: EDSA*

The Landscape Architect requested the client to organize a kick-off meeting with the local community whereby the Landscape Architect interacted with the local Keija community and heard their views on Ecotourism development in their surrounding areas. Several discussions were held during which local wisdom and knowledge was tapped to ensure that valuable information about the region is used to develop a truly authentic ecolodge. The opportunity was also taken to inquire about local bamboo artisans and craftsmen/craftswomen.

Image 2: Consultants meeting with local Keija community members

*Source: Hitesh Mehta*

Before returning to the office, the Landscape Architect also generated an "Opportunities and Constraints" plan which showed all those areas that had great opportunities for development and conservation and all those areas where there was constraint for development.

## 4.2 Physical Site Planning and Landscape Design

Once the analysis has been carried out, the next stage is to prepare a Site Plan for the selected property. Physical Site planning as a process of creating the built environment. Site Planning is defined as the "art of arranging structures on the land and shaping the spaces between" (Lynch et al., 1984)

Site planning in landscape architecture and architecture refers to the organizational stage of the landscape design process. Site planning involves plans for specific developments in which precise arrangements of buildings, roadways, utilities, landscape elements, topography, water features, and vegetation are shown. This is done by arranging the compositional elements of landscape, buildings and paving planting, and water in site plans (Tyler et al., 2011). Regulation, markets, and local community cultures also demand that site planning operates with careful consideration of wider, off-site natural and human environments.

The Chinese based the science and art of siting and orienting buildings upon the workings of earth forces, which are known as Feng Shui, literally "wind" and "water". Rooted deeply with ecology, hydrology, geology, and astronomy, Feng Shui aims to harmonize nature with the built environment (Eitel, E. ,1988). Feng Shui offers an ancient method of site planning that adds to balance and harmony for those who live on the land and for the earth itself (Mehta H et al., 2002). All-natural shapes in the landscape have meaning to the Chinese and correspond to the ground qualities that they reflect. Feng Shui is a widely practiced concept for site planning in China, Korea, and Japan. It is in Pearl River Delta South China (close to the location of Crosswaters Ecolodge) and Hong Kong where Feng Shui is practiced more than any other region in the world (Matthews, M., 2019).

It is important to understand that Feng-Shui is a cultural phenomenon that is beyond the judgement based on scientific understanding. Neither despising it as superstition nor promoting it as a science will reveal its true essence. Feng Shui has its deep meaning in human knowledge and cultural ecology. Understanding the profound meaning of Feng-Shui plays a significant role in knowing Chinese people and Chinese culture; in understanding the landscape and its spirit; in improving and creating modern landscapes with more meaning (Kongjiang & Yu, 2019). The designer should respect and understand the owner's beliefs in their landscape models. This requires that designers understand feng-shui and its meaning in landscape at a higher level. For this project, the Landscape Architect researched over five books on Feng Shui philosophy.

## *Best Practice Applied Research: Site Planning and Landscape Design*

Before starting work on the Site Plan, the landscape architect visited some of the iconic Feng-shui planned projects like the Qing dynasty Summer Palace and Forbidden City in Beijing. He also visited and researched both the Suzhou Gardens in China and Kyoto Garden in Japan.

The Landscape architect involved the local people in the planning process from the start so that they could tap into the local wisdom and knowledge of the Keija tribe to develop the site into a true ecolodge. Members of the local council and leading citizens from the main village have made valuable contributions. There has been significant community participation in the preparation of the Crosswaters Ecolodge plan and we received regular feedback on the various plans and designs.

For the metaphysical site planning, the Landscape Architect brought in a local renowned Feng Shui master with 20 years' experience to help analyze the 'chi' (Chinese word for energy) of the site. South China is the center of Feng Shui beliefs and thought processes and the Landscape Architect felt that the local cultural and spiritual values needed to be respected. It was crucial that the 'chi' of the site is not disturbed during development. The Feng Shui Master analyzed the initial Feng Shui inspired preliminary plan that had been created by the Landscape Architect and which had the entrance Bamboo bridge, reception, lounge, dining area, conference hall and spa buildings located along the feng-shui 3O of N-S axis. This is like the axis of the Summer Palace pavilions in Beijing.

Image 3: A feng shui master (in the foreground) analyzed the preliminary master plan and provided invaluable input on the energy flows of the site and directions of the main axis of the project (below left).

*Source: Hitesh Mehta*

Figure 5: A feng shui audit of the Preliminary Master Plan

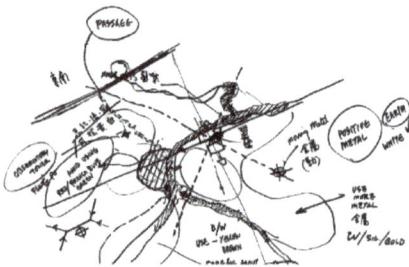

Figure 6: Feng shui calculation tables for the site

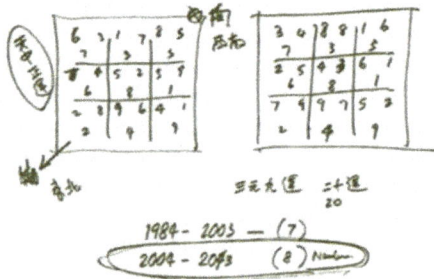

*Source: EDSA*

All the villas and other public buildings were sited in the most desirable feng-shui configuration with the hills in the back and the water to the front. The 'chi' that flows through all the buildings is harnessed using walls that keep the 'chi' from escaping. Crosswaters Ecolodge was the first rural hospitality project in China designed using Feng-shui principles.

Figure 7: The Cross Waters Ecolodge site plan follows "feng-shui' principles with the main buildings situated along a "3 degrees of magnetic north' axis.

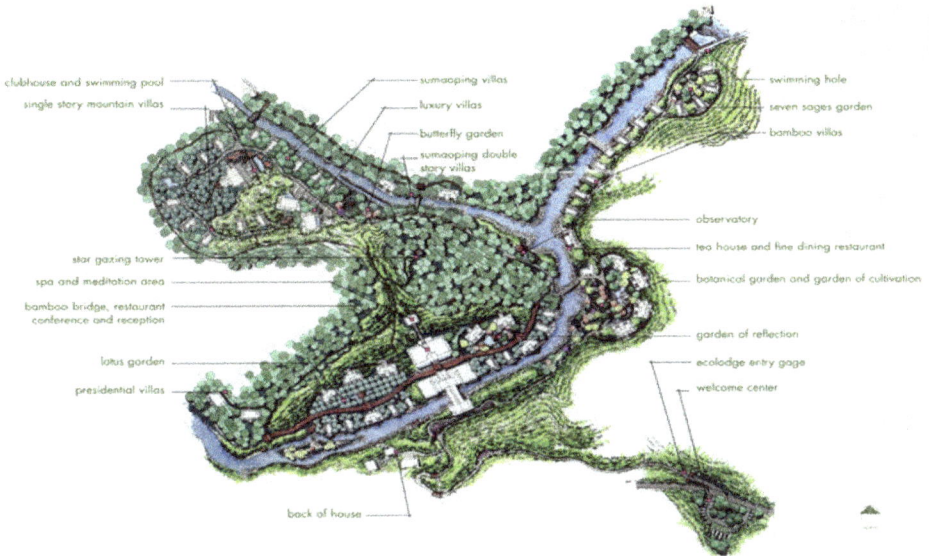

*Source: EDSA*

The site planning and Landscape Design of Crosswaters Ecolodge also celebrates the **rich garden** history of China. The Landscape Architect **researched and analyzed** ancient Chinese gardens i.e., Tao, Suzhou and Qing Dynasty Imperial Gardens I.e., Summer Place, Forbidden City to understand the relationships between inside-outside and cosmic orientations of buildings and gardens. This research was then used in the planning and design of the various gardens. The botanical garden will showcase Bamboo Species from China and act as an interpretive experience for guests. Other gardens include a Lotus Garden, a Reflective Moon Garden, Longevity garden, Water Lily Garden, a Seven-Sages Tao Garden, a Sculpture Garden, and a Garden of Cultivation (Vegetable and Fruit Garden). It should be noted that all plant species specified for the project are native to the region and that there are no exotic species.

An understanding of Chinese garden design elements led to research into the poetics of traditional Chinese garden design. Each one of the garden spaces in Crosswaters site has its roots in cultural history and poetry of the country. Combined with existing site conditions made for a one-of-a-kind outdoor culturally connected experience. For example, the Seven Sages of the Bamboo Grove design is based upon an old Taoist story about a group of poets, musicians and scholars that would gather next to a rushing river in a dense bamboo grove to discuss philosophy whilst drinking wine.

Figures 8a-8d: The Seven Sages Garden is a "continuity of the vernacular" representation of Taoist history.

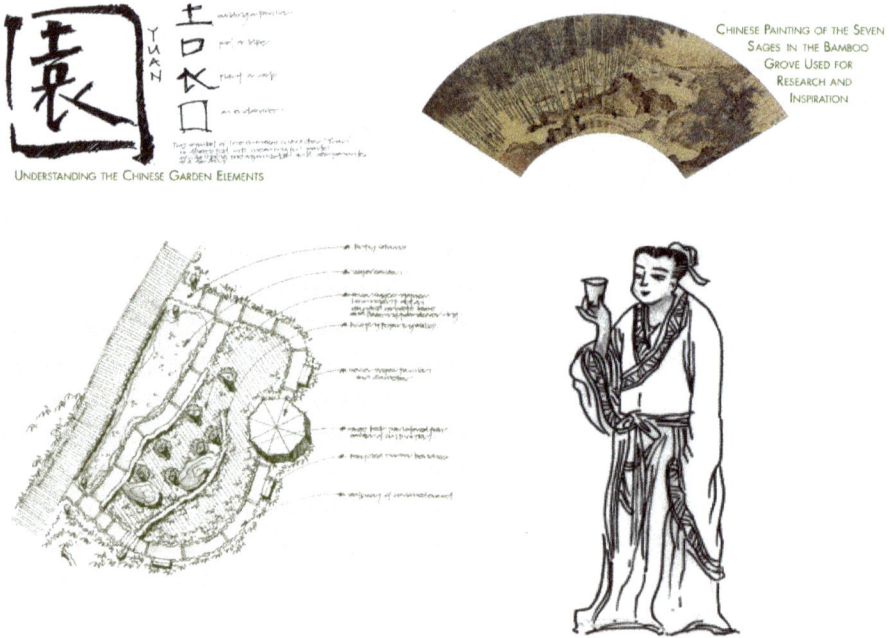

UNDERSTANDING THE CHINESE GARDEN ELEMENTS

CHINESE PAINTING OF THE SEVEN SAGES IN THE BAMBOO GROVE USED FOR RESEARCH AND INSPIRATION

*Source: EDSA*

## 4.3 Building Culturally Inspired Architectural Forms and Spaces

The use of traditional local materials and available resources and the incorporation of many bioclimatic features in the design of the traditional settlements give them a sustainable identity. Through their historic diversity, quality and continuity, the traditional settlements constitute non-renewable resources. Sustainable development approaches offer a new platform for the integration of the crucial aspects of cultural heritage into a larger social and economic strategy (Philokyprou, M., 2015)

The climatic and sustainable design elements that characterize vernacular architecture using locally available materials, environmentally friendly methods and simple architectural forms should constitute the source of inspiration for ecolodge architects. The "sense of place' created by vernacular architecture has often been dismissed as accidental, but today we recognize in it, an artistic form that has resulted from human creativity (Rudofsky, 1984). The philosophy and practical knowledge of this 'architecture without architects' should be used as an untapped source of inspiration for the design of ecolodges.

Researching local construction techniques is an important aspect for ecolodges. The Architect should study local construction methods and materials right from the beginning and create a database of construction and craft skills available locally. It would then be prudent to use the construction technology and improvise it to meet market demands but still be easy for locals to use.

## *Best Practice Applied Research: Culturally Inspired Architectural Forms and Spaces*

The Crosswaters Ecolodge project had five architects working on the various aspects of the project. The architects responsible for the concept design immersed into the local Keija culture and studied and analyzed their Architecture in Shangping Village to look for inspiration. The various sketches below demonstrate the sense of place created by the construction techniques used to build the walls, doors, windows and roofs of the Keija Houses. The individual elements of architecture and unique construction details helped to become a guiding force in establishing character and style that was unique but also reflected the elements that made this region special.

Figure 9a and 9b: Study of Vernacular Architecture

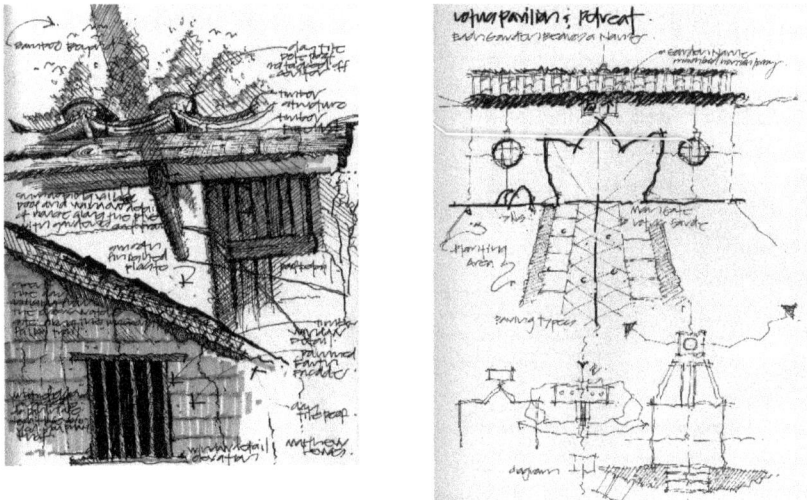

*Source: EDSA*

The Architects used their analytical research on local Architectural Forms and created a 'continuity of the vernacular' architecture which utilized Lo-TEK. The orthogonal layouts of local buildings meant that not one single building in Crosswaters was organic in plan. And the typology of form of the ecolodge villas was borrowed from the forms found in Keija farm buildings and the architectural floor layout of the Wellness Center was inspired by the typical courtyard Keija house. The only difference being that the central court in the wellness center has a covered roof and that the internal spaces are being used for a hospitality wellness function.

Image 4: Vernacular Architecture

Image 5: Ecolodge Architecture

Image 6: Vernacular Architecture

Image 7: Ecolodge Architecture

*Source: Hitesh Mehta*

As with Keija vernacular architecture, Crosswaters Ecolodge was constructed with mostly organic materials found in and around the site. There has been extensive use of abundant local materials such as bamboo, earth, marble and river stones. These materials, along with local construction techniques were used to creating stone walls, rammed earth walls, and roofs. Two elderly local craftsmen (between 70 and 80 years old) identified during the site analysis trip, were brought in to help with the rammed earth walls and mentor younger colleagues in the art of this type of wall construction. Some of the other materials were recycled materials boardwalks are made of abandoned railway ties; clay roof tiles are from buildings demolished by local people in the village.

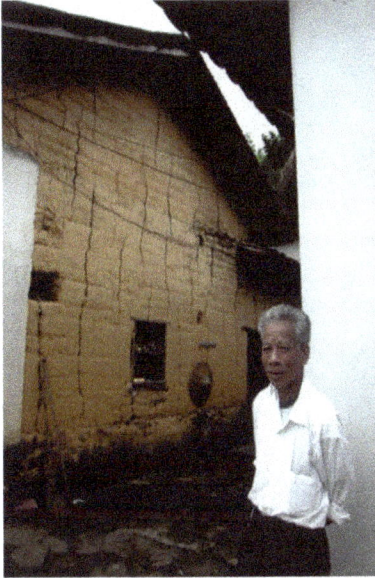

Image 8: Old man in village who built his house with mud in 1985

Image 9: Lo -TEK building the Ecolodge Villa rammed-earth wall

*Source: Hitesh Mehta*

The architecture and interior design of the lodge has continued the vernacular in its form and spatial relationships. And by doing so, has created an architecture that is timeless.

127

Image 10: Timeless architecture and landscape design

*Source: Hitesh Mehta*

# Conclusions

Despite all the challenges, if project owners can find the right environmental, social and financial balance, they can reap big rewards from sustainable tourism projects. Ecotourism is one of the fastest-growing tourism niches, and it will continue to influence the rest of the tourism products (i.e., Nature tourism, adventure tourism, mass tourism etc.) for years to come (GEN, 2015).

**5 Major Key Takeaways:**

- In our field, the best results are achieved when you have practiced ego-less design with an eco-full approach! Employ a bottom-up approach to planning to empower communities and local consultants and bring to the drawing table, local people, and consultants on day one of the planning and design process. Never look into imposing your designs/ego onto a landscape. Use your six senses to immerse into the landscape and then lightly place your buildings so they harmonize rather than dominate.
- Do your homework and research about lessons learnt by others. Visit a few properties and learn about the do's and don'ts. Also read

books on case studies on how other hotel owners have embraced sustainability and created a profitable business.

- Make sure you have a good group of consultants whose heart is in the right place and who also want to make a difference. Collective creativity. Select architects, interior designers and landscape architects with proven records in sustainability.
- Do the 'cradle to cradle' research on building materials. There is loads of great information on the internet. Compare prices. Check out reviews.
- Education and awareness are the key to making change. Spend time to educate clients and local communities and be patient.

# REFERENCES

Alexander. C. (1979). *The Timeless Way of Building*. New York: Oxford University Press,

Anyamba T.C., & Adebayo A.A. (1993). *Traditional Architecture: settlement, evolution, and built form*. Nairobi: Jomo Kenyatta Foundation.

Aysan, Y.F. (1988). *An understanding of the 'Vernacular Discourse'*. Oxford: Oxford Brookes University.

Berkes F. (1999), *Sacred Ecology* 2nd Edition. New York, NY: Taylor & Francis.

Berkes F., Colding J., & Folke C. (2000). "Rediscovery of Traditional Ecological Knowledge as Adaptive Management." *Ecological Applications*, Vol. 10, No. 5 pp. 1251-1262: Ecological Society of America Stable.

Buday Richard. (2017). The Confused and Impoverished State of Architectural Research. Retrieved from https://commonedge.org/the-confused-and-impoverished-state-of-architectural-research/ .

Congress on The European Architectural Heritage. (21 - 25 October 1975). The Declaration of Amsterdam. Retrieved from: https://www.icomos.org/en/and/169-the-declaration-of-amsterdam .

Eitel, E. J. (1988). *Feng-Shui: The science of sacred landscape in old China*. Tucson, Arizona: Synergetic Press.

Epler Wood, Megan. (2002). *Ecotourism: Principles, Practices and Policies for Sustainability*. Paris: UNEP.

Essawy, Sally. (2017). "The Timelessness Quality in Architecture." *International Journal of Scientific & Technology Research Volume 6, Issue 02*. New Delhi.

Ganju, M.N. (2016). "Documentation and conservation of vernacular architecture: conservation and continuity," Pages 484-490. *International Journal of Environmental Studies*, Volume 73 Issue 4: Taylor and Francis

Garroute, E. (2006). *Anthropology: Appreciating Human Diversity*. New York: McGraw Hill Education

Global Ecotourism Network (GEN). Retrieved from: https://www.globalecotourismnetwork.org/what-it-is-not-ecotourism/

Hawkins, D.E., Epler Wood M., & Bittman, B. (1995). Ecolodge Sourcebook for Planners and Managers. Burlington: The Ecotourism Society

ICOMOS 12th General Assembly. (1999). Mexico: Charter on The Built Vernacular Heritage.

International Ecolodge Forum 2. (1995). Puntarenas, Costa Rica: The Ecotourism Society.

Kongjiang, Y. (2019). *Ideal landscapes and the deep meaning of Feng Shui: Patterns of Biological and Cultural genes*. San Francisco: Oro Editions.

Lynch, K., Hack G. (1984). *Site Planning*. Cambridge: MIT Press

Matthews, M., (2019). *Feng Shui: Teaching About Science and Pseudoscience*. New York: Springer International Publishing.

Mehta H., (2007). *Towards an Internationally Recognized Ecolodge Certification, Quality Assurance and certification in ecotourism*. Rosemary Black and Alice Crabtree (eds) – CABI.

Mehta, Hitesh (1999). "International Trends in Ecolodges." Paper presented at the 1999 World Ecotourism conference and field seminar. Kota Kinabalu, Malaysia: The International Ecotourism Society.

Mehta Hitesh (2010). *Authentic Ecolodges*. New York: Harper and Collins

Mehta, H., Baez, A., & O'Loughlin, P.(eds) (2002). *International Ecolodge Guidelines*. Burlington, Vermont: The International Ecotourism Society.

Nimsamer P., & Walliman N., (2014). "Continuity and Change of Thai vernacular building tradition in Thailand." In Mariana C., Gilberto C., Sandra K., (Eds). *Vernacular Heritage and Earthen Architecture* (Pgs. 239-244). Florida: Taylor and Francis Group.

Oliver Paul. (2005). *Encyclopedia of Vernacular Architecture of the World*. Cambridge: Cambridge University Press.

Philokyprou M. (2015). "Continuities and Discontinuities in the Vernacular Architecture." *Athens Journal of Architecture* Volume 1, Issue 2 (Pages 111-120)

Rudofsky, B., (1964). *Architecture Without Architects: A Short Introduction to Non-Pedigreed Architecture*. Albuquerque: University of Mexico Press.

Russel D., Bottril C., & Meredith G., (1995). "International Ecolodge Survey." In Dr. Hawkins D., Epler Wood M., & Bittman S. (Eds), *Ecolodge Source Book for Planners and Developers*. Burlington: The Ecotourism Society.

Dr. Rössler M., (2018). *Overtourism in UNESCO World Heritage Sites*. Tourism Watch: UNESCO World Heritage Centre.

Tyler, N., & Ward R., (2011). *Planning and community development: A guide for the 21st century*: Norton & Co.

Fact Sheet (Feb. 2011). *Traditional Ecological Knowledge for Application by Service Scientists*: U.S. Fish and Wildlife Service.

Watson, Julia., (2019). *Lo-TEK Design by Radical Indigenism*. Italy: Taschen GmBH.

China's Post-Olympic Woe. Retrieved from https://www.npr.org/2012/07/10/156368611/chinas-post-olympic-woe-how-to-fill-an-empty-nest.

Interview with Hitesh Mehta: The Spiritual Side of Sustainability. (2017). Retrieved from: https://sustainability-leaders.com/interview-hitesh-mehta/: Sustainability Leaders Project.

An interview with Hitesh Mehta: The Guru of authentic ecolodge. (2016). Retrieved from: https://businessmirror.com.ph/2016/10/31/an-interview-with-hitesh-mehta-the-guru-of-authentic-ecolodges/ Interview by Mina Gabor: Business Mirror.

Chapter 7

# Affective Reunions: Ethics and Politics of Enslavement Memorialization Travel

*Natália Marques da Silva, PhD Candidate*
*Global & Sociocultural Studies*
*Florida International University*
*Miami, Florida, US*

## Introduction

As the chapters in this book attest, tourism is an important avenue for discovery and exchange. By travelling, we expose ourselves to different pockets of the world, and by extension, different pockets of ourselves and our past. The entire experience, from planning a trip to discussing what we saw and learned with friends and family, can be deeply profound. However, not all forms of travel serve the same purpose. While some adventures are embarked on for rest and relaxation, others propel travellers into challenging situations, memories, and locations. This includes memorialization travel, where the present interlaces with highly bewildering and lingering pasts. Travel to remember the Transatlantic Slave Trade, for example, despite overlapping with some aspects of general tourism, such as when travellers rest in a hotel or visit a restaurant, is typically a highly emotive undertaking that is quite distinct from casual travel. In its entirely, the process may inspire more questions than answers, though it may also bring peace and resolution. And for descendants of enslaved persons, it may bring closure through the veneration of ancestors and persons not yet mourned, encounters with homeland, and exchanges with diasporic kin.

In this chapter, we examine how travel shapes different components of enslavement memorialization. Enslavement memorialization is the commemoration of memories, heritages, and histories related to peoples who were enslaved as well as locations and events associated with slavery. Memorialization, whether public or private, elaborate or simple, physical or spiritual, demonstrates diverse ways people engage, negotiate, and frame the past. While memorialization itself can take place anywhere, anytime, and through various manifestations, enslavement memorialization travel entails visiting specific sites and/or attending location-based events. Though travellers' expectations and experiences vary (see Hartman, 2008; Holsey, 2008; Reed, 2014), this form of travel can be immensely transformative. That is because as a lens to the world, travel has become an important vehicle for confronting the

Transatlantic Slave Trade and its aftermath, as well as parallel forms of oppression. To understand how this takes place, we begin by considering different travellers' associations and motivations, followed by an overview of travel stages, and some considerations on representation, affect, and narrative. Questions to consider include: What are the opportunities and limitations of enslavement memorialization travel? Or more broadly, to which degree does travel enable engagements with the past?

## Travelers and Travel Destinations

Travellers vary in their motivations for memorialization and in their association with legacies of enslavement. Kwame Essien (2016), in speaking about descendants' travel to Ghana, lists several potential motivations, including to "reconnect with the spirits of their ancestors, to gain emotional healing for the atrocities that were committed against their ancestors, to find meaning to many unanswered questions about their roots, and as emotional renewal for their battered souls" (Essie, 2016, p. 241). These activities, while replete with opportunities for resolution, healing, and community (Hartman, 2008; Holsey, 2008; Pierre, 2012; Rahier, 2020; Reed, 2014), may be accompanied by painful experiences. Descendants may come face to face with spaces and instruments of terror, visualize or embody ancestors' pain, and oftentimes, because this past is unresolved and continues to reverberate, encounter situations and spaces that too closely resemble contemporary iterations of violence and racism (Huggins, 1995). Despite the painful possibilities that lurk within memorialization, (Hartman, 2008; Holsey, 2008; Reed, 2014), the potential for veneration and reflection strengthens many descendants' resolve to pursue enslavement memorialization travel.

Contributing factors to the pursuit of enslavement memorialization travel also include the opportunity to 'reunite' with ancestors as well as diasporic kin. Whether through a Pan-Africanist affiliation or other global circuits of Blackness (Hintzen and Rahier, 2010; Schramm, 2010), these travellers identify with descendants' plight and the weight of this shared history. In a study of Black visitors to Castle-Dungeons in Ghana, for instance, Jean Muteba Rahier (2020) demonstrates that shared racialization experiences can transcend borders. These visitors stand in solidarity with descendants or, as Bayo Holsey (2008) illustrates in a study of the same region, find additional meanings in their association with enslavement history.

Descendants of slave owners or traders, in contrast, may travel in search of restitution and atonement. In one such travel, Edward Ball (1999), whose family participated in enslaving thousands of people, undertook a journey across the U.S. South and parts of West Africa to come to terms with his family's past. In regards to his journey, Ball stated: "I felt accountable for what had happened I also felt shame about the broken society that had washed up when the tide slavery receded" (1999, p. 14). Travel became one of Ball's (and others') main avenues for directly confronting this history and the white privilege that accompanies it. Of course this is not true of all descendants of enslavers or peoples who have directly benefited from enslavement, some of whom have not sought reinstitution or forgiveness, a matter that can cause friction as travellers' of various motivations encounter one another at different destinations (Holsey, 2008; Reed, 2014).

This list of traveller associations and motivations is not exhaustive. Some travellers are multi-affiliated (i.e., their ancestry includes both slave owners and enslaved persons) or might stem from communities where enslavement is not openly discussed (Bellagamba, 2012). Motivations for travel may also overlap other forms of travel such as Personal Heritage Tourism or Roots Tourism and therefore include additional components, such as homecoming and diasporic exchange, travelling to learn more about enslavement, travelling on behalf of those who cannot undertake a journey themselves, or travelling to produce a cultural product, such as a book, film, or art. And finally, travellers might be motivated by their desire to visit specific destinations or participate in location-based events.

## Remembering Enslavement

Travellers' itineraries might include visiting museums and memorials, heritage sites (such as ports, holding cells, and castle-dungeons) and natural sites (rivers, shores, forests, clearings, and so forth) that are meaningful to enslavement memories, heritages, and histories. As **sites of slavery** (see Knowledge Box), these spaces are embedded in layered histories that narrate and represent the past from different perspectives. Some, such as the Musée Ogier-Fombrun in Haiti, specialize in specific places or events in this case, the Haitian Revolution while others, such as the National Museum of African American History and Culture in Washington, D.C., discuss enslavement amidst a much broader history. Older sites, such as the Elmina and Cape Coast Castle-Dungeons in Ghana, whose earliest versions were erected in 1461 and 1555 respectively, have served different functions over time, and thus carry alternative meanings to different visitor groups (Abaka 2012; Thiaw, 2008).

As remembrance destinations, some sites of slavery may be sought for their symbolic or cultural significance rather than historical or archaeological value. This is the case of Juffure, a Gambian village whose popularity as a remembrance destination is credited to Alex Haley's (1976) *Roots: The Saga of an American Family* (Wright, 2011). Juffure is characterized in the book and in the subsequent television series (1977 and 2016) as the birthplace of Kunta Kinte, an alleged ancestor of Haley who becomes enslaved. Though segments of this narrative have been since questioned by scholars (Courlander, 1984; Wright, 2011), Juffure remains an important destination for memorialization. Another example is Gorée Island, in Senegal. The popularity of Gorée as a remembrance destination is contested by some due to histories the site highlights or obscures through curatorial processes (Thiaw 2008; Tillet 2009). However, as Ibrahima Thiaw (2008) proposes, negotiation over a site's narrative and meaning do not prevent it from becoming "powerful symbol in African and African American memories of the Atlantic slave trade" (Thiaw, 2008; p. 45). The keywords in Thiaw's statement are *symbol* and *memories*, both of which contribute to this (and other) sites' ability to foster remembrance and to stand for a past that altogether spans several centuries across numerous locations, therefore rendering it fluid and unbound to limitations of time and space.

## Knowledge Box: Sites of Slavery

Pierre Nora (1989) developed the term *lieux de mémoire*, or sites of memory, to signify a space whose meanings derive from shared interpretation of the past. In writing about Nora's work, Salamishah Tillet (2012) explains: "sites of memory preserve those aspects of the past that uphold national identity and then legitimate and transmit those histories to present and future generations" (p. 4-5). To expand this concept further, Tillet draws on Nora's *lieux de mémoire* and Toni Morrison's work on slave autobiographies to consider "sites of slavery," or "objects, texts, figures, places, and narratives from the American past that provide tangible links between present-day Americans and American chattel slavery" (p. 5). This concept transposes the physical realm, whereby tangible and intangible entities coalesce with discourse, narrative, and memory. As such, sites of memory, or in this case, sites of slavery, are ever-changing and always reflexive of societal revision. In this chapter, we expand this concept once more by considering locations *and* associated entities, and amplifying the term to include not only Americans and American chattel slavery, but the broader examples of enslavement and their various meanings to peoples across the African continent and its Diaspora.

In addition to destination-based travel, travellers might also plan their trip around special events. Nominal location-based examples include Ghana's bi-annual PANAFEST (1990s-Present) and Benin's Ouidah Festival (1990s), both of which have influenced large-scale diaspora/continental gatherings (Price, 2001; Holsey, 2008). Meanwhile, international holidays, such as the United Nations' International Day for the Abolition of Slavery (December 25), and national holidays, such as Juneteenth (June 19) in the United States or *Dia Nacional da Consciência Negra* (November 25) in Brazil, supply travellers with multiple potential destinations as several locations prepare simultaneous celebrations. Common threads in memorialization events include veneration rituals, diasporic exchanges, homecoming celebrations, cultural performances, research presentations, and outings to local sites.

Whether one is travelling alone, with a group, or to join a gathering; to a single location; multiple destinations; or through physical or digital means, enslavement memorialization itineraries illustrate the diverse ways travellers engage the past. In the following section, we examine how some of these engagements manifest in different stages of travel.

# Stages of Travel

There are three important stages in travel journeys: the beginning (planning, preparing, anticipation), the middle (travel experiences), and the end (return, reflections). Scholars vary in their interpretations of the middle stage, interpreting it as one long stage or breaking it down into primary and secondary destinations or separating the beginning as pre-planning and departure (see Olivier and Botha, 2003). However organized, understanding travel stages is essential to studies on travellers' experiences. During pre-travel, travellers may dedicate ample time and resources to planning their trip while reflecting on their expectations, anticipations, or pre-conceptualizations about a destination or planned activity. As the travel itself unfolds, travellers' experiences shift between the mundane and the profane (Graburn, 1989), and vary given their itinerary, travel conditions, and experiences. In post-travel, travellers may reflect on their experiences, reminisce with keepsakes, photos, and videos, and share their memories with others. This stage may repeat indefinitely and may eventually be undertaken by others as travel experiences transcend from a traveller's memory into a group's collective memory (Silva, 2020). Ultimately, all stages contribute to visitors' narratives about their experience. According to Jacqueline Tivers and Tijana Rakic (2012) "narratives about travel and tourism are not only an essential ingredient in the construction of personal, collective, and place identities but are also important in the process of contemplating, experiencing, remembering and disseminating travel and tourism experiences" (2012, 1). As such, when shared with others, in addition to shaping a traveller's own recollections, they influence future travellers as well as the development of destinations, facilities, services (such as tours, events, and so forth). During enslavement memorialization travel, these stages are critical to travellers' experience and may be accompanied by unique encounters with **affect**, a "body's *capacity* to affect and to be affected" (Seigworth and Gregg, 2010, 2, emphasis in original) by surrounding stimuli. In the following sections, we draw from travel writings by Black authors from the Diaspora to highlight some of these stages and ways different descendants have memorialized enslavement.

## Pre-Travel Anticipation

During the planning stage or while in-route to their respective destinations, travellers may anticipate upcoming experiences or expectations. Depending on the destination, the trip may constitute a *homecoming*, or a return to one's ancestral home. This may be specific, as in returning to the precise birth-place of one's parents or grand-parents, or general, as in returning to a region or continent. Homecoming, as an integral component of diaspora identity-making (Clifford, 1994; Schramm, 2010), produces additional expectations. Prior to coming home, return travellers may visualize images amassed through collective memory, popular media, school, or pre-travel research (Hartman, 2002; Schramm, 2010; Zeleza, 2010); or wonder how they will be received (Hadley, 2006; Holsey, 2015).

They may also contemplate their motivations for travel, and the questions and answers they hope to address. As he embarked on a long-term trip across the African continent, for example, journalist Eddy L. Harris (1993) reflected on his travel motivations: "I hardly knew what I was looking for, except perhaps to know where home once was, to know how much of me is really me, how much of being black has been carried out of Africa" (Harris, 1993; p. 138). Harris' statements point to a yearning in personal heritage / roots tourism to seek answers about one's past, or how the past contributes to one's personhood. His comment about wanting "to know where home one was" is a critical component of this journey that is directly related to the roots, routes, and ruptures of the Transatlantic Slave Trade (Gilroy, 1993; Hall, 1994; Glissant, 1997). Despite considerable advancements in genealogy, historical archives, and other research tools, many descendants lack knowledge of ancestors' names and origins.

The anonymity of scores of enslaved persons is a contributing factor for identity-based travel (travel to find oneself), and lack of information on other details of ancestors' lives (personality, experiences) may elicit visualization and contemplation of ancestors' potential journeys. In pre-travel, particularly if the destination is continental Africa, descendants' thoughts may be in the Middle Passage, and whether their own journey constitutes as a *reverse* Middle Passage. In the final chapter of *Roots* (1976), discussed in an earlier section of this chapter, Alex Haley recounts boarding a ship to The Gambia. The experience, as demonstrated by the following excerpt, prompted Haley to (re)member Kunta while making his own trip across the Atlantic:

> After each late evening's dinner, I climbed down successive metal ladders into her deep, dark, cold cargo hold. I lay on my back on a wide rough bare dunnage plank and forced myself to stay there through all ten nights of the crossing, trying to imagine what did he see, hear, feel, smell taste and above all, in knowing Kunta, what things did he think? (Haley, 1976, p. 584).

In forcing himself to stay in an unadorned plank each night of the crossing, Haley drew from discomfort to confront unanswerable, unknowable elements about the past. Comparing and contrasting one's own transatlantic voyages with the Middle Passage is an important element of return travel. Often, it means affective reunions between ancestors and descendants pre-date one's arrival at a respective destination, a matter that for many returnees, greatly shapes the remainder of their trip.

## Travel Experiences

During her first trip to Ghana's Cape Coast Castle, a major destination for enslavement memorialization travel, Seestah IMAHKÜS (1999) remarked: "As I stood transfixed in the Women's Dungeon, I could feel and smell the presence of our ancestors. I felt tightness at the base of my scalp as though someone had grabbed me by the back of my neck, causing me to fall to my knees" (1999, p. 212). IMAHKÜS' visceral reaction entailed the paralyzing effect of entering a space where thousands of African women and young girls were once held, followed by an ephemeral encounter. To better understand this phenomenon, we must consider the micro and macro sociohistorical contexts that inform enslavement memorialization travel. At the micro-level, there are specific events and conditions associated with particular destinations. In this case, the violence and dehumanization endured within the Women's Dungeon. And at the macro-level, there are the forces and circumstances that enabled and facilitated this brutality and its aftermath at countless locations. These factors contribute to travellers' experiences at enslavement memorialization destinations, which as vestiges of the Transatlantic Slave Trade, have great symbolic, cultural, and historical meaning. For these reasons, it is not surprising that in travel accounts, particularly when visualizing how people were treated in ships, holding cells, prisons, and plantations, travellers report responses such as fear, sadness, anger, despair, and guilt (Holsey, 2008; Reed, 2014).

At times, the weight of these emotions can be so great as to prevent or delay engagement with certain sites of slavery. In writing about the same site IMAHKÜS had visited, for example, Maya Angelou (1986) recounted an attempt to drive past the dungeon: "Despite my hurry, history had invaded my little car. Pangs of self-pity and sorrow for my unknown relatives suffused me. Tears made the highway waver and were salty on my tongue I had to pull off the road. Just passing near Cape Coast Castle had plunged me back into the eternal melodrama" (1986, p. 118). Angelou, who was living in Ghana at the time, described listening to friends' recollections of the site, but needing to delay her own visit due to the weight of enslavement history and the challenging emotions it can elicit.

To be clear, these are not the only parameters of travellers' responses, which overall can also include contentment, peace, and optimism. By the end of IMAHKÜS' visit, for instance, the debilitating feelings she first endured were transformed into reconciliation. She stated: "as I knelt crying and terrified, a warmth slowly crept across my shoulders, the fear that had previously wretched my gut was replaced by a feeling of serenity and calm I had never experienced before" (IMAHKÜS, 1999, p. 212). Throughout the course of IMAHKÜS' visit, the Women's Dungeon, initially a place of horror, expanded to include the possibility of healing. Alongside the aforementioned emotions, IMAHKÜS now found peace, or in her words, "serenity and calm." After permanently relocating to Ghana, IMAHKÜS has gone on to guide other returnees through the Dungeons, stating that although "each time was different, each time it hurt" as descendants released their sorrow by crying, screaming, or praying (IMAKÜS, 1999, p. 144).

The affective experiences described in the writings of IMAHKÜS and Angelou do not imply that sites of memories elicit such responses among all visitors. For some, for example, Ghanaian castle-dungeons did not lead to similar experiences. Saidiya Hartman (2008), a scholar and descendant who spent a year in Ghana, relayed of her visit to Elmina Castle-Dungeon:

> I had entered the dungeon intending to do all the fine things stated in the marble plaque posted at the entrance: commemorate the dead, remember the anguish of the ancestors, and prevent such crimes against humanity from ever happening again. But five minutes in the underground dashed these grand aspirations. The stark facts won out—it was a hold for human cargo and knowing what happened here couldn't remedy oblivion or betoken a brighter future or lessen the suffering of the dead (Hartman, 2008, Chapter 6).

In contrast to IMAHKÜS, Angelou, and other visitors, the sombre setting did not elicit the same responses in Hartman, who instead encountered affective memorialization through other means. By visiting living communities whose oral histories and cultural performances depict resistance and kinship, Hartman appears to have found some of the answers or cathartic experiences that she had not found in the Dungeons. In *Lose Your Mother* (2008), Hartman ends her travel recollections with the following depiction:

> The young man standing next to me offered to translate. He said something that I couldn't hear because of the girls' song. I shook my head to indicate that I didn't understand what he had said. He moved a few inches closer to me and then shouted in my ear. The girls are singing about those taken from Gwolu and sold into slavery in the Americas. They are singing about the diaspora. Here it was—my song, the song of the lost tribe. I closed my eyes and I listened (Hartman, 2008, Chapter 12).

Thus far, the travel experiences relayed in this section have focused on Ghana, a destination that has attracted not only a lot of travellers but a lot of travel writing due to its symbolism, popularity, and length of memorialization and homecoming projects (Holsey, 2008; Schramm, 2010; Reed, 2014). However, as the opening of this chapter indicates, memorialization is not bound by geography. For a final example of enslavement memorialization travel, we turn to the writings of N. Fadeke Castor (2017), a scholar and practitioner of the Ifá/Orisha faith. In the following excerpt, we learn about a gathering to honour ancestors somewhere in the Trinidadian coast. The description takes us full circle from the beginning to the end of a ritual that starts with unsurmountable pain but closes with some resolution:

> [W]e were going to honor and appease those lost souls who perished during the Atlantic slave trade, both on land and at sea, but especially those who had lost their lives at sea. I gazed out at the horizon and mused that if I could see all the way beyond the horizon. A wave of sorrow washed over me. I felt their screams, the pain of collective souls left to wander so far from home. And I screamed. I howled. I cried and writhed, bawling, knowing that this recognition as not enough. It could never be enough. And I rose with my

body covered in dirt and my face covered in salt, from the waves and from my tears. I knew then that we had made an important step in honoring those spirits who had felt forgotten and whose souls had never been put to rest (Castor, 2017, p. 154).

Castor's journey points to the cycle of venerating people who lost their lives to a treacherous system of violence. The phrase "it could never be enough" points to the challenges of (1) venerating *all* who perished through this system; and (2) knowing veneration might not undo the pain they must have underwent. Nonetheless, veneration remains "an important step." In addition to bringing peace and resolution to descendants, who may perform such rituals on a regular basis, it is a means to provide funeral rites for people whose passing might not have been acknowledged during their own lifetime. Lastly, it underscores spiritual components that drive many descendants' motivations for memorialization.

Collectively, these examples of enslavement memorialization travel demonstrate different ways travellers engage with the past, and some of the responses such activities can elicit. In the next section, we discuss examples pertaining to post-travel recollections.

## Post-Travel Recollections

As discussed earlier in this chapter, the completion of a trip might lead travellers to reflect on their experiences; share stories and souvenirs with family, friends, and colleagues; recount their trip through art, film, music, poetry, or other creative outlets; reminisce with keepsakes; and/or plan future trips. The experience may repeat often or happen once in someone's lifetime. In communities where few can travel, recounting one's journey may contribute to a groups' collective memories as its members imagine someone else's journey as their own (see Silva, 2020). While for some these processes may lead to resolution, for others it is an unresolved stage of ongoing contemplation. Harris' homecoming, for example, ultimately produced more questions than answers: "I was trapped Africa was so long ago the land of my ancestors that it held for me only a symbolic significance. Yet there was enough to remind me that what I carry as a human being has come in part from Africa. I did not feel African but was beginning to feel not wholly American anymore either. I felt like an orphan, a waif without a home" (Harris, 1993, p. 137-138). For Harris, travel opened an indefinite state identity-making and unmaking as he reflected on how travel affected him.

In his own travel and migration writings, Philippe E. Wamba (1999) addressed Harris' predicament as a necessary process of reconciliation. In the following excerpt, Wamba touches on travel outcomes as diaspora and continental Africans grasp their shared histories:

African Americans have long sought to derive a sense of self, identity, and pride from their conceptions of Africa and Africans, to develop an antinode to the disoriented rootlessness of a person who slave masters insisted were orphans of a shameful and brutish motherland. And Africans have at various moments in history looked to blacks in America with a similar sense of identification and fraternity, hoping for and offering assistance and support, and identifying and exploring real and imagined commonalities. These potent passions and their lively interplay have fuelled cultural innovations, political partnerships, rich mythologies, empowering social movements, and **international systems of travel, exchange, circulation**, and **recycling** in which black voyagers, writers, leaders, activists, and artists constructed a transatlantic black kinship. (Wamba, 1999, p. 28, emphasis added).

Travellers and those who receive them throughout their journey contribute to, as Wamba states, "international systems of travel, exchange, circulation, and recycling" (1999, p. 28) that facilitate remembrance, memorialization, and community. Post-travel is a critical stage in this venture: it is a reflexive time period whose products outlive travel itself. In the next section, we consider the challenges and opportunities that shape and are shaped by post-travel and the stages that precede it.

## Politics of Memorialization

In studies about enslavement memorialization travel, as well as diaspora travel, personal heritage tourism, roots tourism, and other forms of travel, scholars raise questions about over-commercialization of events and experiences, contested narratives and representation, and tensions and uneven power relations among travellers, local residents, and people in the heritage and tourism industries (Bruner, 2005; Holsey, 2008; Reed, 2014; Schramm 2010). Addressing these issues is crucial to ensuring enslavement memorialization destinations and gatherings are sustainable, ethical, and safe. Otherwise heritage and travel professionals run the risk of traumatizing or retraumatizing visitors, unknowingly instigating conflict, or failing to provide a safe environment. While there is no 'one fits all' approach to memorialization, the topics discussed below serve as an overview of some of the politics entangled in this form of travel—and by extension—the destinations and gatherings related to it. Note: *if you do not work or intend to work in the heritage or travel industries, consider the following scenarios from the perspective of a traveller and the way visitors affect or are effected by one another during travel.*

First, a downside to developing destinations and events for travellers is the potential of over-commercialization. In addition to overshadowing the sensitive nature of enslavement memorialization, capitalizing on memorialization for profit rather than pursuing sustainable ventures threatens the integrity of heritage sites, degrades trust between travellers and locals, negatively impacts the natural environment, and/or shifts needed resources into the tourism sector (Schramm, 2010; Handley, 2016). At the heart of this issue is the exploitative potential of tourism. As Hartman (2002) states in an earlier work:

> Longing and loss figure centrally in the strategies of roots tourism—the loss of one's origins, authentic African names, progenitors, and ancestral land all act as impetus to visit, shop, and purchase. Tourism slakes longing, exploits loss, and proffers a cure by enabling cathartic and tearful engagements with the era of the slave trade. (Hartman, 2002, p. 760).

Countering this perspective are sincere gestures between travellers and hosts. In writing about Ghana, Ann Reed (2014) highlights some examples: "African Americans and Jamaicans (among others) have not only participated in pilgrimage tours; some of them have contributed to community-based development, provided schools, and made long-term investments" (Chapter 1). Hartman and Reed's respective statements point to paradoxes in enslavement memorialization: the capacity of tourism as a positive development tool versus the potential of exploitation, particularly during venerable travel. The tenuous relationship between collaboration and exploitation necessitates continuous evaluation and reflection by all parties involved (travellers, professionals, funding agencies, etc.). As many of the chapters in this volume and in other types of publications attest, transparency and ethics are keystones of equitable and sustainable travel.

Another element to consider is that monetization also impacts narrative and representation. In some cases, descendants of slave owners and traders have capitalized on monuments to profit from a reframing of their ancestors' past (Araujo 2012; Rice 2010). Funders may also have a say on how slavery is depicted in media, events, or sites of memory, at times obscuring history to please one group or another (Bellagamba 2012; Hasty 2002; Schramm 2007; Wright 2011). In some cases, altering history or preferring some perspectives over others reveals deep set inequalities rooted in slavery and its aftermath. The following example illustrates this point as well as the power of affective narratives. In a number of plantation museums across the Southern United States, visitors and tourists learn about chattel slavery, pre-abolition Antebellum society, and the U.S. civil war. Although these are important topics to disseminate, visitors are generally more likely to hear detailed accounts about the lives, lifestyles, and belongings of slave owners and overseers than about slavery and the people they enslaved (Benjamin and Alderman 2018; Hanna 2008; Modlin, Alderman, Gentry 2011). Furthermore, information about slave owners and overseers tends to be shared with greater emotion and for longer periods of time than information on enslaved persons, whose personalities, lives, and plights become obscured by the former (Modlin, Alderman, and Gentry; 2011). As a result, underinformed visitors and travellers may walk away from the experience with a tilted view of slavery (Araujo, 2010; Capdepón, Sierp, and Strauss 2020).

Travel destinations may also unintentionally aggregate travellers and visitors with conflicting perspectives. Not all who visit a site of slavery are there to memorialize.

Some may end up at a location randomly, out of curiosity, due to a group itinerary, or out of a requirement (such as a work training or university course). Generally, persons in this group respect others' rights to memorialize, though sometimes they may find amusement in a site's content; laugh, mock, or insult exhibits and visitors; deflect blame and accountability; and/or become violent (Bruner, 2005; Hartman, 2008; Holsey, 2008; Reed, 2014). Though the potential of such exchanges is demoralizing, they demonstrate the ongoing need to address this painful history from multiple vantage points, including the provision of safe forums for discussion and exchanges. It is an important role that travel and travel destinations play in drawing attention to discord and the extent to which they can facilitate reconciliation. As Marcus Wood (2000) states of memorials, museums, and heritage sites, "the historic trauma of transatlantic and plantation slavery must not be encapsulated within a history believed to be stable, digested and understood; this history is also *not over*, and is *evolving*" (Wood, 2000, p. 11, emphasis in the original). Directly and indirectly, enslavement memorialization travel contributes not only to descendants' journeys and ancestors' remembrance, but also to counter amnesia, apathy, and racism through resilience, open-dialogue, and anti-racism.

## Conclusion

As this chapter demonstrated, enslavement memorialization travel produces complex engagements with the past. Whether participating in a one-time ritual or following a lengthy trajectory, travellers (re)member ancestors, both known and unknown to bear witness to crimes and horrors that must not be repeated. By witnessing, they ensure this difficult past is not forgotten by current and future generations. After all, "the past that is not past reappears, always, to rupture the present" (Sharpe, 2016, 9), and as such, ramifications that remain unresolved go on to produce needless pain and suffering.

When pursued ethically and mindfully, travel accelerates this process as people from different corners of the world come together in community. Exchanges brought about by travel are not always immediately fruitful. Confronting this painful, unresolved past and its mark in an ever-tumultuous present is sometimes met with frustration and resentment among different groups, particularly as people reckon with divergent interpretations of the past (Hartman, 2008; Holsey, 2008; Reed, 2014; Handley, 2016). However, travel remains an important mechanism for meaning-making, community-building, and self-discovery as we learn from, with, and about one another. Journey by journey, we stand closer with one another and hopefully a brighter tomorrow.

## Four Major Takeaways

1. Enslavement memorialization travel entails visiting one or more locations to honour peoples, memories, heritages, and histories associated with enslavement. For descendants it can also entail homecoming and meeting diasporic kin.

2. Motivations for this type of travel include veneration, reflection, and restitution, though traveller's expectations and experiences vary.

3. Stages of travel also vary and may produce strong emotive and affective experiences as travellers engage with a deeply painful past.

4. As an unresolved legacy, enslavement is a critical yet challenging matter to represent and narrate. Industry professionals must be mindful of balancing divergent perspectives with safe environments that foster healing, open-dialogue, and community.

# REFERENCES

Abaka, E. (2012). *House of Slaves and 'Door of No Return': Gold Coast/Ghana, Slave Forts, Castles & Dungeons and the Atlantic Slave Trade*. African World Press.

Angelou, M. (2010). *All God's Children Need Traveling Shoes*. Random House.

Araujo, A. L. (2010). *Public Memory of Slavery: Victims and Perpetrators in the South Atlantic*. Cambria Press.

Ball, E. (1998). *Slaves in the Family*. Farrar, Straus and Giroux.

Bellagamba, A. (2012). "Reasons for Silence: Tracing the Legacy of Internal Slavery and Slave Trade in Contemporary Gambia". In A. L. Araujo (Ed.), *Politics of Memory: Making Slavery Visible in the Public Space* (pp. 35–53). Routledge.

Benjamin, S., & Alderman, D. (2018). "Performing a different narrative: Museum theater and the memory-work of producing and managing slavery heritage at southern plantation museums." *International Journal of Heritage Studies*. 24(3), 270–282.

Bruner, E. M. (2005). *Culture on Tour : Ethnographies of Travel*. University of Chicago Press.

Capdepón, U., Sierp, A., & Strauss, J. (2020). "Introduction: Museums and Monuments: Memorials of Violent Pasts in Urban Spaces." *History & Memory*, 32(1), 5–8.

Castor, N. F. (2017). *Spiritual Citizenship: Transnational Pathways from Black Power to Ifá in Trinidad*. Duke University Press.

Clifford, J. (1994). "Diasporas." *Cultural Anthropology*, 9(3), 302–338.

Courlander, H. (1984). "Kunta Kinte's Struggle to be African." *Phylon*, 47(4), 294–302.

Essien, K. (2016). *Brazilian-African Diaspora in Ghana: The Tabom, Slavery, Dissonance of Memory, Identity, and Locating Home*. Michigan State University Press.

Gilroy, P. (1993). *The Black Atlantic: Modernity and Double Consciousness*. Verso.

Glissant, É. (1997). *Poetics of Relation* (B. Wing, Trans.). University of Michigan Press.

Graburn, N. H. H. (1989). "Tourism: The Sacred Journey." In V. L. Smith (Ed.), *Hosts and Guests: The Anthropology of Tourism* (Second, pp. 21–36). The University of Pennsylvania Press.

Haley, A. (1976). *Roots: The Saga of an American Family*. Doubleday.

Hall, S. (1994). "Cultural Identity and Diaspora." In P. Williams & L. Chrisman (Eds.), *Colonial Discourse and Post-Colonial Theory: A Reader* (pp. 222–237). Harvester Wheatsheaf.

Handley, F. J. L. (2016). "Back to Africa: Issues of hosting 'Roots' tourism in West Africa." In Jay. B. Haviser & K. C. MacDonald (Eds.), *African Re-Genesis: Confronting Social Issues in the Diaspora* (pp. 20–31). Routledge.

Hanna, S. P. (2008). "A Slavery Museum? Race, Memory, and Landscape in Fredericksburg, Virginia." *Southern Geographer*, 48(3), 316–337.

Harris, E. L. (1993). *Native Stranger: A Black American's Journey into the Heart of Africa*. Vintage Books.

Hartman, S. (2002). "The Time of Slavery" *The South Atlantic Quarterly*, 101(4), 757–777.

———. (2008). *Lose Your Mother: A Journey Along the Atlantic Slave Route*. Farrar, Straus and Giroux.

Hintzen, P. C., & Rahier, J. M. (2010). "Theorizing the African Diaspora: Metaphor, Miscognition, and Self-Recognition." In P. C. Hintzen, J. M. Rahier, & F. Smith (Eds.), *Global circuits of blackness: Interrogating the African diaspora* (pp. ix–xxvi). University of Illinois Press.

Holsey, B. (2008). *Routes of Remembrance: Refashioning the Slave Trade in Ghana*. The University of Chicago Press.

———. (2015). "Embodying Africa: Roots-Seekers and the Politics of Blackness." In H. A. Baker & K. M. Simons (Eds.), *The Trouble with PostBlackness* (p. 144). Columbia University Press.

Huggins, N. I. (1995). *Revelation: American History, American Myths*. Oxford University Press.

IMAHKÜS, S. (1999). *Returning Home Ain't Easy but It Sure is a Blessing*. One Africa Tours & Specialty Services.

Modlin, E. A., Alderman, D. H., & Gentry, G. W. (2011). Tour Guides as Creators of Empathy: The Role of Affective Inequality in Marginalizing the Enslaved at Plantation House Museums. *Tourist Studies*, 11(1), 3–19.

Munroe, L. (2016). "Constructing affective narratives in transatlantic slavery museums in the UK." In D. P. Tolia-Kelly, E. Waterton, & S. Watson (Eds.), *Heritage, Affect and Emotion: Politics, practices and infrastructures* (pp. 114–132). Routledge.

Nora, Pierre. 1989a. "Between Memory and History: Les Lieux de Mémoire." *Representations* (26): 7–24.

Pierre, J. (2012). *The Predicament of Blackness: Postcolonial Ghana and the Politics of Race*. The University of Chicago Press.

Price, T. Y. (2001). "The Return: Slave Castles and the African Diaspora." In *Afrocentricity and the Academy: Essays on Theory and Practice* (pp. 187–1998). McFarland & Company, Inc.

Rahier, J. M. (2020). "Affect and the Memorialization of the Slave Trade: Spontaneous Expressions of Synchronic Global Black Consciousness in the Visitors' Books at Elmina and Cape Coast Castles, Ghana." In R. Corr & J. Fewkes (Eds.), *Private Lives, Public Histories: An Ethnohistory of the Intimate Past*. Lexington Books.

Reed, A. (2014). *Pilgrimage Tourism of Diaspora Africans to Ghana*. Routledge.

Seigworth, G. J., & Gregg, M. (2010). "An Inventory of Shimmers." In G. J. Seigworth & M. Gregg (Eds.), *The Affect Theory Reader* (pp. 1–26). Duke University Press.

Silva, N. M. Silva, N. M. (2020). "Journey to Cacheu: Africa as Homeland to the Quilombola Territories Santa Rosa dos Pretos, Filipa and Santa Joana." In *Kwanissa: Revista de Estudos Africanos e Afro-Brasileiros*, 3(6), 32-55.

Schramm, K. (2010). *African Homecoming: Pan-African Ideology and Contested Homecoming*. Taylor & Francis.

Sharpe, C. (2016). *In the Wake: On Blackness and Being*. Duke University Press.

Thiaw, I. (2008). "Every House has a Story: The Archaeology of Gorée Island, Senegal." In L. Sansone, E. Soumonni, & B. Barry (Eds.), *Africa, Brazil and the Construction of Transatlantic Black Identities* (pp. 45–62). African World Press.

Tillet, S. (2009). "In the Shadow of the Castle: (Trans)Nationalism, African American Tourism, and Gorée Island." *Research in African Literatures*, 40(4), 122–141. JSTOR.

_____. (2012). *Sites of Slavery: Citizenship and Racial Democracy in the Post-Civil Rights Imagination*. Duke University Press.

Tivers, J., & Rakic, T. (2012). "Introducing the Narratives of Travel and Tourism." In J. Tivers & T. Rakic (Eds.), *Narratives of Travel and Tourism* (pp. 1–8). Ashgate Publishing.

Trouillot, M.-R. (1995). *Silencing the Past: Power and the Production of History*. Beacon Press.

UNESCO. (2014). *The Slave Route: 1994-2014. The Road Travelled*.

Wood, M. (2000). *Blind Memory: Visual Representations of Slavery in England and America 1780-1865*. Routledge.

Wright, D. R. (2011). "The Effect of Alex Haley's 'Roots' on how Gambians remember the Atlantic Slave Trade." *History in Africa*, 38, 295–318.

Zeleza, P. T. (2010). "African Diasporas: Toward a Global History." *African Studies Review*, 53(1), 1–19.

# Conclusion: Creating a New Tourism post Covid

*Carolin Lusby*

In times of structural change and uncertainty (such as the global pandemic) we are faced with a decision: To rebound with similar structures, or rethink how we operate. So often, times of crisis and uncertainty feel uncomfortable for us, and we aim for a quick return to a sense of normalcy. For tourism, this might mean a return to the status quo of the industry whenever possible, and to recreate the model of uncontrolled mass tourism experienced pre pandemic. And yet simultaneously, we are forced to face a new reality of individual and global circumstances and characteristics that demand change, one of them being obvious health and social distancing measures now implemented by tourism businesses globally. As we reflect on new societal and individual demands, we have to also acknowledge a deep rooted need to focus on the well-being of people and planet. In that sense, this book argues that it is insufficient to rebuild tourism with solely health measures. Instead this volume argues that now is the time to create a more conscious, balanced and ethical industry.

For one, tourism in and of itself is a vital force of and for well-being. The pandemic, while shutting down the industry, has simultaneously brought the importance of self-care, individual well-being and resilience to the forefront. When we stay well and centered, we are resilient and able to rebound. How can we stay well and sane in a world that seems unpredictable and saturated with oftentimes conflicting, negative, and at times false, information? A slower, more conscious form of travel has been embraced by many to escape some of these pressures. Travel in that sense teaches us how to embrace change and stay flexible and adaptive. It also aids in finding meaning in current and past happenings, so as to confront these issues with new hope and certainty. Travel also aids in finding purpose and self, as could be seen in the chapter on memorialization travel. An increasing ethic of conscious consumption is furthermore shifting the tourism industry.

Focusing on quality, as opposed to quantity, of tourists in that sense is an imperative rule for tourism to stay sustainable and not overpower destinations. As mentioned in the chapters on cultural tourism in Havannah, and the Overtourism chapter, various forms of mass tourism decrease visitor satisfaction and lead to less return travel. As such, focusing on limiting tourist numbers, not only makes sense as a post pandemic health measure, but also to improve visitor satisfaction and ensure that residents are not overlooked, and negatively impacted. Another proven factor in increasing well-being is connection to nature and spending time outside. Chapters in this volume have shown that a focus on interpretation and conservation of natural attractions increase guest satisfaction. In that way, tourism allows for conservation of natural resources, while aiding in overall well-being of planet and people, when managed properly. The chapter on vernacular architecture has shown how a focus on local knowledge and design can create outstanding ecolodges that conserve and celebrate local cultural and natural resources. Many studies have shown the economic viability of natural attractions as a way to sustain livelihoods through tourism dollars over the long-term. Elephants in Africa, fish in the ocean, or hectares of forest are all resources tourists will pay directly and indirectly to enjoy. As such they benefit local stakeholders economically as well in the long haul, as opposed to one time consumption.

Lastly, research has shown repeatedly that a sense of altruism, or giving back, has positive effects on happiness and well-being. This explains why forms of volunteer tourism, which fill the basic human need to connect, give back and make a difference, have risen so dramatically in popularity. The chapter has shown how this sudden jump in demand has led to an at times unethical approach to the delivery of volunteer tourism experiences, where the wants and needs of travelers are prioritized. The chapter gave tips for travelers and organizations to provide meaningful and ethical experiences instead, acknowledging the fantastic contribution volunteer tourism could make to the well-being of travelers and local communities, if managed properly. A top down approach to tourism was also visible in architectural design pre-pandemic, where building plans were oftentimes conflicting with local architecture. The chapter on vernacular design called for a more balanced and locally focused approach to design, giving specific examples and tools. The chapter on inter-culturalism has shown the importance of cultural awareness in travelers to navigate guest -host interactions and cultural gaps successfully to the benefit of all involved. In that way travel opens new horizons and increases intercultural understanding. Previous research has shown that these benefits can be achieved when travelers are given opportunities to interact with hosts in meaningful one -on- one interactions, as opposed to staying in the tourism bubbles described in chapter one. Tourism then is a vital tool to create meaning, intercultural understanding and increase well-being. The examples in this book showed select ways of reaching these goals with a newly balanced, more conscious approach to managing tourism, which prioritizes well-being of communities, planet and people while being financially viable.

Now, more than ever, we are conscious of the interconnectedness of all. Viruses as well as ideas travel at light speeds, reaching even the remotest corners of the world. In that way, our actions and thoughts create global realities. We are indeed creators, and not just bystanders. As such, tourism enterprises and travelers are aware of the impacts of individual acts. So often in the past, individual profit was valued over collective well-being. As negative consequences were shared by many, and individuals were still to gain from exploitative acts, the industry engaged in unethical behavior to profit certain players.

In this new age of global connectedness, the urgency to act with an ethic of global well-being is a dire call to action for tourism stakeholders and players. It is not enough to rebuild tourism structures as is, merely adjusting safety and health protocols. We need an industry responsive to the demands of the global community, natural resources and travelers. What does that mean? First and foremost, it means telling the stories that need to be told and putting up to date information out there. Educating travelers on the impacts of their choices by providing them with up to date information. In terms of traveler demands, it could mean an industry focused on allowing for a deeper connection to self, other cultures and nature. It could also mean an industry that allows for immersing oneself in new destinations for extended periods of time through hybrid work/travel settings. We also need an industry that creates a sense of safety through transparency and up-to-date information. For the global community, this means the industry's focus should be on sustainability, local communities and environmental conservation. In that sense, policies should reflect safeguarding and restoring cultural and natural resources. The narrative of the past does not have to be the story of tourism's future. We can re-create the story of tourism. Our baseline for what is healthy does not need to be what we currently see. What if, through tourism dollars and volunteers, we can recreate coral reefs, re- plant forests, restore torn structures? What if, through travel we examine our own cultural values and as a result demand cultural change? Policies and benchmarks can be set to restore and create a new future. Travel is an essential human activity and will continue to enrich lives and communities if we approach it with an ethic of a fair and balanced development.

www.ingramcontent.com/pod-product-compliance
Lightning Source LLC
Chambersburg PA
CBHW050809270326
41926CB00026B/4651